CLASSIC RUM

In the same series:

CLASSIC RUM

JULIE ARKELL

First published in 1999 in Great Britain by
Prion Books Limited
Imperial Works
Perren Street
London NW5 3ED

© PRION BOOKS LIMITED
Text copyright © Julie Arkell 1999
Designed by DW Design

A CIP record for this book is available from the
British Library

ISBN 1-85375-298-3

Cover design: Bob Eames

Printed and bound in China

CONTENTS

INTRODUCTION

Today's press would have us believe that rum has become "the new vodka" – the latest drink for trendy socialites who may be seen flocking to the rum bars springing up daily in the world's most fashionable capitals. To rum aficionados, however, this must seem somewhat amusing.

For a start, rum is hardly new – it's been part of history for more than three hundred years. And the notion of rum bars being a thoroughly modern invention will surprise anyone who has visited the Caribbean – the islands are packed with everything from posh pubs to ramshackle huts dedicated to the pursuit of rum-drinking. And they've been there a long time.

Some say that vodka is the most popular spirit in the world; others say rum. While there's no doubt that Bacardi is the best-selling individual spirit brand in the world, it's unlikely that anyone will ever establish the wider truth. Travel to any rum-producing country and you stumble across men swigging rough rum from unlabelled plastic bottles. Where does this come from? Does a local distiller supply it or is it unrecorded moonshine?

One of the joys of rum is that it comes in an array of richly diverse guises. It's easy to say that rum is the distilled product of fermented molasses or sugar cane juice, but there is a world of difference between an unaged, fresh-from-the-column-still white rum that you drink with cola and a pot still-produced, golden rum, aged for years in oak casks and deep with nuances of flavour. They are two totally different drinks.

Things are complicated further still when one explores cultural attitudes. In Mexico, for instance, rum is usually consumed "straight up" while most of Europe sees it as a mixable spirit. In Central Europe, rum is rarely perceived as a premium product and the Spaniards claim Cuban rum to be the only genuine article. Not to mention the fact that in the Caribbean rum is sprinkled on a new baby's forehead, that Jamaicans believe in the topical healing properties of rum, or that rum plays a significant role in Haitian voodoo ceremonies.

Julie Arkell, 1999

HISTORICAL HIGHLIGHTS

WHAT'S IN A NAME?

It is thought that the name "rum" was first coined in Barbados, although no one really knows how or when it originated. Compared with some of the more exotic language used to describe it in the past, however – rumbustion, Barbados water, red-eye, rumscullion, Devil's death and rumbo – "rum" sounds rather dull.

And what about "Kill-Devil", as English author Richard Ligon aptly described Bajan rum in the 1640s when rum was so crude and strong it could "overpower the senses with a single whiff". Indeed, as Ligon wrote, "It lays them to sleep on the ground!" – permanently in many cases.

Ten years later, another idiom appeared in a report written by an anonymous visitor to Barbados: "The chiefe fudling they make in the Island is Rumbullion, alias Kill-Divill, and this is made of sugar cane distilled, a hott, hellish and

terrible liquor." Rumbullion was already part of the Devonshire dialect at this time, used to describe "a great tumult", which speaks for itself if the rum was anything like as vile as these old writings suggest.

Nelson's Blood is yet another lovely epithet, gleaned from the widely held belief that Nelson's body was brought back to England in a barrel of rum. In truth, the cask was filled with brandy but either way he's said to have had a smile on his face.

Above

A sugar cane plantation in the 1800s – one of many that sprung up throughout the West Indies in the wake of colonisation.

EARLY DAYS

If Christopher Columbus could take a peek at the Caribbean today, he'd probably be amazed. The cane cuttings he took to the New World in 1493 were planted to make sugar. He could not have foreseen that they would eventually give rise to a drink that was to dominate the West Indian economy.

There's no doubt that the Caribbean was the birthplace of the modern-day rum industry but historical evidence supports the theory that a prototype rum had been made much earlier elsewhere.

Sugar cane grew like a weed in China and India two thousand years ago and, following his conquest of the Punjab, Alexander the Great's armies spread the "reed which gives honey without the help of bees" throughout Egypt and the Mediterranean. Some eight centuries later, sugar cane was introduced into Europe by the Moors who were certainly adept at turning it into spirit, having learned the art of distillation from the Saracens.

This knowledge was transferred to the Caribbean by the Spanish Conquistadors in the 16th century. When their hopes of finding gold were dashed, they turned instead to making their fortune from rum which, ironically, became almost as valuable as the treasure they had originally sought. Meanwhile, the Dutch and Portuguese established settlements in Brazil, turning sugar manufacture into a flourishing industry. Before long, they were producing a spirit from the molasses, although at that point only the native Indians and African slaves would touch it.

With the English, French and Dutch colonisation of the islands of the eastern Caribbean during the 1600s, rum quickly became a cornerstone of the Caribbean economy. It was often more profitable than the sugar used to make it and it had the added bonus of encouraging naval ships to stay in the islands to ward off plundering pirates.

Above

Columbus, whose gift of cane cuttings to the Caribbean has led to this now worldwide industry.

THE SLAVE TRADE

Why did all-creating Nature
Make the plant for which we toil?
Sighs must fan it,
Tears must water,
Sweat of ours must dress the soil.
Think ye Masters, iron-hearted
Lolling at your jovial Boards,
Think how many Backs have smarted
For the Sweet your Cane affords!

COWPER'S NEGRO COMPLAINT

From a 1791 pamphlet published in an attempt to persuade the British to abstain from West Indian sugar and rum to promote the abolition of the slave trade

The burgeoning sugar cane plantations required intensive cultivation and the advantages of using slave labour to carry out the bitter and crippling work soon became apparent to the colonists. The demand for slaves fuelled the infamous triangular trade route in which almost a thousand vessels were engaged at any one time. Ships would leave England bound for the west coast of Africa where goods were bartered with local African rulers for slaves who were then transported under horrendous conditions to the Caribbean. Here, the human cargo would be exchanged for rum and agricultural goods needed back in England, thus closing the triangle.

Above
The boom of the sugar and rum industries was only made possible by the terrible exploitation of human life – the slave trade.

RUM IN THE ROYAL NAVY

Life aboard the old men-of-war was extremely primitive, made crueller by a lack of anything to drink besides sour beer or foul water stored for long periods in wooden casks.

When Vice-Admiral William Penn captured Spanish Jamaica in 1655, local rum was taken on board. The Jack Tars must have welcomed this sweet-tasting alleviation of the misery and hardship of life before the mast.

By 1731, the daily rum issue to all hands was common practice in ships squadroned in the West Indies. At first, rum simply replaced the beer ration which meant that each sailor was drinking half a pint of very crude and very strong rum every day, swallowed neat in one gulp. Intoxication was inevitable, causing many accidents in the rigging and losses overboard. Before long, ship's surgeons were suggesting that rum and sailors did not mix: "It impaired their health, ruined their morals and made them slaves to every brutish passion."

Opposite
"Up Spirits" on
H.M.S. COVENTRY,
Christmas, 1941.
The introduction
of a daily rum
ration in the
17th century
greatly improved
morale and
living conditions
aboard ship.

In 1740, the respected Vice-Admiral Edward Vernon ordered rum be no longer served neat but diluted four-to-one with water. Furthermore, it was to be served in two half-issues a day. This order has been described by the Victualling Department of the Ministry of Defence as "perhaps the greatest improvement to discipline and efficiency ever produced by one stroke of the pen". Vernon's nickname of "Old Grogram" (from the unusual material of his boat-cloak) was shortened by the sailors to "grog" as the name for the new ration.

Over the years to follow, grog became even weaker and, in 1850, the proportion of neat rum in the ration was decreased to half a gill, a quarter of the original allowance.

With technological advances and the growing sophistication of weapons systems, the Royal Navy finally decided to abandon the daily rum ration altogether. On July 31, 1970, "Black Tot Day", mock funerals were held and black armbands worn and, at Six Bells of the Forenoon, the very last "Up Spirits" was piped.

AN AMERICAN TALE

A General Court Order made in Connecticut in 1654 confiscated "whatsoever Barbados liquors, commonly called rum, Kill-Devill or the like". Nevertheless, rum soon became an important part of the colonial North American economy. Pork, beef, dried fish, flour, livestock and pine logs were traded for West Indian rum which was particularly popular with the fishermen and lumberjacks who had to endure the harsh northern winters.

Despite its being illegal, rum was also sold to the American Indians who drank vast quantities of it. Indeed, alcohol abuse devastated the social and economic order of many of the Indian communities that had already been ravaged by European diseases. Never mind the Cavalry; rum alone wiped out whole tribes. Interestingly, this brought about one of the most important temperance movements in American history: many tribal leaders banned the drinking of rum within their communities. However, their efforts to halt the trade in rum within the Indian community as a whole proved powerless. It took the American Revolution, and the disruption of the colonial economy which came in its wake, to slow down the trade in what historian Peter Cooper Mancall describes as "deadly medicine".

Before long, molasses was being shipped directly to New England for distillation into rum and hundreds of distilleries sprang up. A roaring trade developed and an estimated 12 million gallons of rum were being enjoyed each year.

Most of the molasses came from the French islands because it was cheap. In 1733, however, parliament in London passed the first Molasses Act, imposing prohibitive taxes on the import of all molasses, rum and sugar from non-British islands of the Caribbean. The new law was not welcomed in the colonies as the raw materials of the British islands were far more expensive. It is even held by many historians that rum played as important a role as tea in the discontent that led to the Boston Tea Party in 1773.

Some scholars also suggest that rum altered the course of American history in quite a different way. According to historian Charles Taussig, when legendary hero Paul Revere embarked on his midnight gallop from Charleston to Lexington, it was simply to warn revolutionary

leaders Samuel Adams and John Hancock to flee
the approaching British troops. But this meant
riding through Medford, the centre of the 18th-
century New England rum trade. Revere stopped
at the home of Isaac Hall, Captain of the
Medford minutemen and proprietor of a thriving
lery. After a refreshing draught of Captain Hall's
Old Medford Rum, "He who came a silent
horseman, departed a virile and vociferous

crusader, with a cry of defiance and not of fear." His noisy departure not only woke the company of minutemen but his words inspired them to take up the cause: they gathered at Bunker Hill to resist the advance of British troops and the result was the first confrontation in the American Revolutionary War. What might have happened had Revere stayed sober can only be guessed at.

Opposite
Loading sugar
for export. New
England was one
of the first areas
to import
molasses from the
Caribbean to
distill their own
rum.

"THE NOBLE EXPERIMENT": THE VOLSTEAD ACT

Illicit rum, smuggled in by the rum-runners, helped to keep American spirits high through the dry years of American Prohibition (1920–33). Bootlegging, which thrived under the control of gangster mobsters, was immensely profitable. A consignment of demon drink bought for 170,000 dollars in Nassau could be worth 2 million dollars on the streets of Chicago. Characters like "Scarface" Al Capone, Bill the "King of Rum Row" McCoy (yes, he of The Real McCoy fame) and Gertrude "Cleopatra of the Rum-Runners" Lythgoe are believed to have made as much as 20 million dollars a year.

CHAPTER TWO

THE MAKING
OF RUM

THE RAW MATERIALS

For some unaccountable reason, I have always been tickled by the knowledge that rum is made from leftovers: with few exceptions, rum is produced from molasses, the final by-product in the manufacture of raw sugar from sugar cane – indeed, in many Caribbean islands, producers are legally required to be sugar refiners first and rum distillers second.

Sugar cane, *saccharum officinarum*, is one of the taller members of the grass family with the potential to grow up to 14 feet high under tropical conditions. In these hi-tech days, of course, much genetic improvement has been made to increase sugar content, or to give disease resistance, for example.

Harvesting takes place by cutting the cane as close as possible to the ground. In some places, the fields are first torched to clear away the dead leaves ("trash") or to drive out snakes, a process which also makes the cane easier to cut. The

Opposite
Scenes of the
sugar industry
from the
Illustrated
London News,
1901 – a sugar
mill in Jamaica.
(top) and
unloading cane
at a sugar mill
in South Africa
(bottom).

method used to do this depends on the size of the farm and the nature of the terrain – hand-cutting by machete is still widely used today, for example, where a farm is too hilly or too small to benefit from mechanisation.

The cane plant regenerates by sending out shoots ("ratoons") which grow into new stalks. As they reach towards the heat and light of the sun photosynthesis creates sucrose that is stored unchanged (unusual, since in most other plants, sucrose is converted to starch).

At the time of harvest, the stems of the cane are spongy and full of moist, richly sweet sap, so the last thing that anyone wants at this stage is rain as it dilutes the sugar content drastically. It is also important that the cut cane is transported to the mill quickly because its quality will begin to deteriorate within 24 hours.

At the mill, the cane is chopped and then passed through a series of rollers and grinders that squeeze out the juice from the stems. The pulverised remains ("bagasse") are often used as fuel and can even be turned into chipboard.

The acidic, green-coloured cane juice ("vejou") is now heated and clarified before being pumped into evaporators which drive off excess water. It is then cool-boiled in a vacuum to create a syrupy mixture from which Grade A sugar crystals are extracted – the kind that we use to sweeten our coffee and tea. The brownish-black liquid that remains is known as light molasses (light in both

Opposite
As with any agricultural crop, it is always more economical and efficient to bring in the harvest by machine.

flavour and colour), often used as a syrup for pancakes or waffles. After a second boiling, the molasses is darker and thicker – generally described as black treacle.

Blackstrap molasses, the stuff from which rum is made, comes from a third boiling and is very thick, sticky, dark and somewhat bitter, though it still contains approximately 55 per cent of uncrystallised sugar along with a large number of minerals and non-sugar compounds essential for aroma and flavour. Approximately 1.5 gallons of molasses are needed to make one gallon of rum.

One exception to the rule is *"rhum agricole"* made in the French West Indies from cane juice or concentrated cane syrup. Here, molasses-based rum is described as *"rhum industriel"* or *"rhum traditionnel"*.

FERMENTATION

Before the molasses or cane juice can be distilled, it must first be turned into an alcoholic liquid by fermentation. This, in essence, is all about yeasts' partiality to sugar – put them in a warm, sweet liquid and they multiply like mad, secreting enzymes that convert the sugar into roughly equal quantities of alcohol and carbon dioxide.

First, a "live wash" with a sugar content of approximately 15 per cent is created by diluting the molasses with water, the quality of which is really important. Cane juice, however, can often be fermented without the addition of water if the

sugar concentration is low enough naturally.

In the same way that sugar cane has been technologically adapted to suit soil and climate, various strains of artificial cultured yeasts are used to contribute to the individual characters of different rums. However, many producers are quite happy to rely on the wild yeasts naturally present in the air to induce fermentation.

In some cases, notably where a heavy, dark style of rum is desired, "dunder" (the residue left in the still) or "limings" (the scum that forms on the surface of the molasses as the sugar is being extracted) may also be added for a more pungent flavour.

Above

A fermentation tank where sugar and yeast react to turn the "live wash" into an alcoholic liquid.

The rate of fermentation can be controlled by temperature and depends entirely on the style of "dead wash" (the fermented liquid) required by the distiller. If he wants a light rum, fermentation can be completed in as few as 12 hours, though a day or two is normal practice. Slow fermentation – which can take up to 12 days – produces a heavier type, especially when the live wash is reinforced with dunder.

On completion of fermentation, the dead wash has an alcohol strength of between 5 and 9 per cent.

DISTILLATION

It seems ironic that the water added to molasses for fermentation is then removed again during distillation. However, this is the ethos of distillation: to separate the alcohol from the water in a dead wash. There is a second objective, however, which is to remove undesirable flavouring agents in the form of esters, aldehydes, congeners and acids, while retaining the favourable ones.

There are two discrete methods employed in rum production: pot still distillation and column or continuous still distillation. In both the principle is the same: when wash is heated, alcohol vaporises at a lower temperature than water and these fumes are collected and condensed to give the spirit.

POT DISTILLATION

Pot distillation is the more traditional and time-honoured practice, tending to be reserved for the production of premium rums of great complexity, subtlety and finesse. Each batch of wash has to be heated up separately and needs careful monitoring, so the process is slow and quite costly as a result.

The dead wash is fed into a circular copper kettle which helps to remove impurities. Heat is applied and, after about an hour, the alcohol begins to evaporate. The vapour is piped to a separate cooler and condensed to give the spirit that, in most cases, is distilled a second time to purify and concentrate it further, yielding a distillate that can contain up to 85 per cent alcohol by volume. The art of the distiller is important because the first and the last of the vapours that come off (the "heads" and "tails") contain many volatile poisons and unwanted fusel-oils. The distiller has to judge when to collect the safe "heart" of the distillate, a highly specialised job.

COLUMN DISTILLATION

In contrast to pot distillation, column distillation allows alcohol to be distilled continuously. This modern technique was introduced into the Caribbean at around the turn of the twentieth century and is quite definitely the more widely used, efficient and economical method, producing a stronger, purer spirit.

29

At its simplest, the construction comprises two columns called the "analyser" and the "rectifier". Thanks to a clever design that utilises the physics of heat exchange, the wash is broken down into its constituent vapours (analysed) in the analyser and the vapours are selectively condensed (rectified) in the rectifier.

In practice, it's possible to control the strength of rum produced in a continuous still because the condensate can be drawn off the rectifier at various heights – the higher up the rectifier, the stronger the spirit and a distillate of 95 per cent alcohol by volume is easily attainable.

Opposite

An antique pot still from the Bacardi distillery.

Below

A modern column still which allows for the more efficient continuous distillation.

Incidentally, the spirit of either distillation method emerges water-white in appearance. Any colour in the finished product comes from wood-ageing and/or caramel.

HEAVY VERSUS LIGHT

One of the fundamental precepts of distillation is that the higher the alcoholic strength of the distillate, the purer it will be. Highly rectified, column-distilled rums, therefore tend to be crisp, clean and dry with subtle aromas and only a whisper of molasses character (some even approach vodka in their neutrality) and are described as "light". By contrast, pot still rums, which cannot be distilled beyond 85 per cent alcohol by volume, are relatively "heavy" in flavouring agents.

As a rule, the slower the fermentation, the heavier the rum because other micro-organisms have the chance to pitch in and work alongside the yeasts, contributing their own set of flavours. They simply don't have time to do this during a rapid fermentation.

AGEING

Opposite
The degree of barrel-charring makes all the difference to the colour and toasty flavours of rum.

Put the new clear spirit into an oak barrel, leave it for a few years or so and there's no doubt that it will improve dramatically. And this does not apply to dark rum only. White rums can benefit greatly, too. Indeed, the first time I tasted an aged white rum, it quite knocked me off my feet! It

didn't seem possible that such an innocent-looking white spirit could harbour such intensely deep, lingering and wonderfully integrated flavours.

Like so many processes, the advantages of oak-ageing were discovered by accident. In the old days, the raw spirit used to be bottled directly from the still which remains more or less true for today's unaged white rums (though it's now more usual to filter and dilute them first). When producers started to make more rum than could be consumed, however, the excess was stored in oak barrels that were also convenient vessels in which to transport the spirit. It was soon noticed that the white spirit soaked up colour and also developed a much superior taste.

Exactly what takes place during the ageing process remains one of nature's best-kept secrets, but the marriage between spirit and wood is magical. The rum saps tannin, flavour and colour from the wood and, because wood is porous, it allows the rum to breathe, causing complex oxidative changes to its chemical make-up.

The age or provenance of the barrel seems to make little difference, though once-used bourbon casks are popular and some are first re-charred on the inside. What *is* known for sure is that a small cask (normally 250 litres in capacity) is crucial to good quality – the smaller the barrel, the greater the oak's influence. Any colour acquired by a rum that is to be sold as a white style is removed by charcoal filtering before bottling.

As a rule, light-type rums are aged for anything from one to three years while heavy-types spend a minimum of three years in barrel. With each passing year, the contents become softer, smoother and more mellow and can age successfully for up to 20 years before starting to lose flavour, providing the climate is cool and damp. It ages much faster in hotter, drier environments and seldom improves beyond seven "tropical" years, one "tropical" year being roughly equivalent to two to three cooler-climate years. Age statements have to be treated with some caution, therefore: yes, the older the rum, the better it will be, but the place of ageing is also of great importance.

Over the years some rum is lost to the atmosphere through evaporation. This is known as the "Angel's Share" though, personally, I prefer the Jamaicans' "Duppy's Share" ("duppy" being Jamaican for a ghost or spirit). In temperate climates this loss accounts for about two per cent of the contents of a barrel annually, but in Jamaica for instance, this figure climbs to six per cent – employees at Jamaica's Appleton Estate say that the duppies claim a larger share there because they know where the best rum comes from! It's quite normal, then, for producers to attempt to slow down the rate of evaporation by diluting the new spirit to about 80 per cent alcohol by volume before ageing. Luckily, the more attractive, subtle effects of oak maturation happen to be extracted at lower strengths.

The cooperage, where the ageing barrels are traditionally fabricated, is filled with the sounds of hammering, a gloriously stirring euphony not unlike the old, rhythmic Caribbean spiritual music. Coopering is an art in itself, although sadly it is disappearing in favour of automated barrel manufacture.

Right
The art of coopering, an ancient trade, is now sadly being replaced by more efficient machines.

BLENDING

The majority of rums are created from a blend of rums of different types and ages, and, in the case of some of the large-volume, international brands, may be made up of rums from different countries of origin. Caramel, spices and flavourings are also added at the blending stage if desired (though the latter can be added before or during distillation).

This is where the expertise of the master blender comes into play. His unenviable job is to ensure that the contents of every single bottle are consistent in terms of both flavour and quality – after all, the consumer expects and demands their favourite brand to taste exactly the same every time he or she buys it. Naturally, the specification of each brand is a well-guarded secret.

Once the various constituents of the blend have been selected and bulked together, they are allowed to "marry" for a while before being reduced to bottling strength by the addition of pure water. Here again, the quality of the water is critical.

Talking of strength, it's always wise to study the percentage alcohol given on the label before tucking into any rum with gusto. Some of them are so incredibly strong that you wouldn't want to breathe over a naked flame having taken even the tiniest of sips!

CHAPTER THREE

CLASSIFICATION OF RUMS

Numerous factors determine the style and character of rum: the nature and origin of the raw materials, yeast variety, water quality, fermentation rate, the type of still used, whether it has been barrel-aged (and, if so, where and for how long), the decisions of the master blender and so on.

It's important to appreciate, however, that many of these factors can be controlled, particularly at the blending stage, which means that producers are able to respond to the most significant influence of all – market forces. Jamaica, traditionally associated with dark and heavy rums, is a great example, since producers there are now distilling a tranche of lighter styles to meet current trends.

Recent years have also seen the launch of a great number of premium rums and flavoured or spiced rums. Again, producers are jumping on the bandwagon to take advantage of market growth.

In the absence of internationally set production standards, each rum-producing country's definition of types and styles varies. There are many variables, but here's a rough guide:

WHITE/LIGHT/SILVER

Clear-coloured, light-bodied and dry rums, generally column-distilled, used as a fairly neutral base for cocktails and mixed drinks. The majority are unaged but aged versions do exist (and lovely they are, too).

GOLDEN/ORO/AMBRÉ

Medium-bodied, slightly sweet rums, made in either type of still, that have spent some time in oak. Colour comes from the wood, though it can be enhanced by the addition of caramel. The flavour is quite strong in mixed drinks and they're also delicious drunk straight or on the rocks.

DARK/BLACK

Usually made in pot stills with medium-to-long ageing in heavily charred barrels. Designed for sipping, these are the very traditional, hugely aromatic and full-bodied rums with flavours that unmistakably proclaim "molasses".

PREMIUM AGED/AÑEJO/RHUM VIEUX

Amber-hued, well-matured rums prized by many connoisseurs above a single malt whisky or top cognac. The motto here is "drink less but drink better". These should be treated as very classy after-dinner drinks served in a brandy glass.

SINGLE MARKS

Very rare rums from single distilleries, often bottled from individual casks, i.e. they are unblended. Because no two casks from the same origin and of the same age mature in exactly the same way, these are very exciting bottlings. Definitely for sipping.

OVERPROOF

Largely white rums usually bottled at 75.5 per cent alcohol by volume. Traditionally the favourite of seafarers and estate workers, providing comfort and warmth against the elements. Much sought after in Europe and North America for blending.

FLAVOURED AND SPICED

Emerging as a real winner with younger drinkers – though they've been around for a hundred years or more. Usually served with mixers or fruit juice.

WEDDERBURN AND PLUMMER

Types of heavy, pot-still Jamaican rums fermented with the addition of dunder. Very strong and powerful with flavours of burnt coffee and just a touch of oak. Used widely in Jamaican dark rum blends, but also good for punches and hot toddies.

CACHAÇA (pronounced kah-shah-sah)

Cane spirit in South America is called *aguardiente de caña* or *cachaça* and, like rum, is produced from molasses, cane juice or a mixture of the two, usually unaged. A multi-million case seller in its domestic market, it's the basis of the *caipirinha* (kai-per-ree-nya), a cocktail made with mashed wedges of fresh lime, sugar and crushed ice.

CHAPTER FOUR

WHERE RUM IS MADE – A GAZETTEER

White sands under a sun-drenched sky, azure seas lapping the shore and a Daiquiri to cool the sweated brow…you can almost hear the steel band playing.

When you think of rum the Caribbean instantly springs to mind. There's no doubt that the West Indies is the spiritual home of rum, but it can be made – and usually is – in any country where sugar cane is grown. In addition, some countries that can't support sugar-cane cultivation bring in molasses to turn into rum, or they import raw rum in bulk for maturation, blending and bottling. And just to muddy the waters further, many countries produce rum by all three methods, even within the Caribbean.

One semi-obscure brand I've come across is distilled in the Caribbean…from imported South American molasses. The raw spirit is then shipped in bulk to England for a year's cool-climate ageing. From there, it's sent to India where it's

Opposite
Palm trees, blue skies and plenty of sun… a rum paradise.

reduced in strength, bottled and labelled before being exported to Australia for sale. This kind of global merry-go-round is by no means exceptional and serves to underline the commonly held view that it's not so much where rum is made that matters, but how.

Scratch the surface of most countries and rum will be found, even if it is simply imported in pre-bottled form for domestic consumption. This chapter is dedicated, therefore, to countries that actually distil the stuff, even if it's just for the locals.

THE CARIBBEAN

ANTIGUA

The climate here doesn't lend itself to sugar cane cultivation, so the plantations and mills are long gone. Rum is made from imported Guyanan molasses and a little is exported. The unique character of Antiguan rum comes from the island's small size and flat terrain which maximise the effect of cooling trade winds, allowing rum to age more slowly.

ARUBA

Very little agriculture is practised here owing to the semi-arid environment. A tiny amount of rum is made for local consumption from imported Guyanan molasses.

BAHAMAS

The Matusalem brand is bottled here, but this is

better known as the site of one of Bacardi's manufacturing plants.

BARBADOS

Settled by the English in 1627, Barbados was producing almost a million litres of fiery Kill-Devil annually by 1650. It was by no means the first country to make rum, but it seems that it was the first country from which it was exported.

Until the end of the 19th century, all Bajan rum was made on the sugar plantations. New laws were introduced, however, that banned the sugar merchants from distilling rum and, in turn, the distillers were banned from bottling or marketing their own products. Even today, the 1,500 small farmers who supply molasses to the distilleries remain completely independent of the rum industry and Mount Gay has been the only distillery to circumvent the no-bottling-or-marketing-your-own-product law by simply setting up a sister company.

Domestic demand is split between Mount Gay, Cockspur and Stade's and statistics suggest that each Bajan man drinks 75cl of rum in 11 days, mostly in the prolific rum shops (there are over a thousand of them) at the centre of community life in the Caribbean. Furthermore, because Bajans aren't wild about adulterating their rum with other flavourings, they're adept at making styles that retain subtlety and finesse.

Right through to independence in 1966,

Above *Interior of Pusser's company store, Tortola, British Virgin Islands.*

Barbados has never been colonised by anybody but the British and the traditional links remain strong. Many of the so-called "British rums", like Lamb's, still use Bajan rums in their blends. However, the Bajan rum ethos has spread far and wide and other principal export markets include Australia, Canada, the Caribbean, Germany, Japan, New Zealand, Sweden and the USA.

BRITISH VIRGIN ISLANDS

Local sugar cane has been used here for centuries but the islands also rely on rum imported from Trinidad. Charles Tobias put Tortola on the map in 1980 when he blended and bottled Pusser's Rum. However, with the sale of the brand to Jim Beam Brands, production was transferred to the States, though some of the blend is still sourced from here.

CAYMAN ISLANDS

No sugar cane but a few blends put together for the locals from imported rums.

CUBA

"The most beautiful land the eyes of man have ever looked upon," said Christopher Columbus of Cuba in 1492, who returned to the island a year later bearing sugar cane. By 1620, there were some 50 sugar refineries, increasing to over a 1,000 following the lifting of heavy taxation on Cuban "*aguardiente de caña*".

Rum had always been the rhythm of Cuban life but Prohibition breathed fresh air into the Cuban rum industry when rich American sophisticates – most famously, Ernest Hemingway – swamped the island in search of alcoholic refreshment.

Today, Havana Club is the only significant brand producing light and delicate rums in keeping with local taste preference. However, no summation of Cuban rum could exclude a mention of the Bacardi and Matusalem companies that were founded on the island, the former creating the prototype white rum.

Below
Ernest Hemingway mixes with the Duke and Duchess of Windsor in Cuba – playground for rich Americans since the thirsty years of Prohibition.

DOMINICA

On the whole the islanders prefer white rum and locally made brands share the market with imported varieties. However, sales from cask – a kind of bring-your-own-bottle-and-we'll-fill-it arrangement – dominate, with local manufacturers providing the unbranded contents.

Moonshine, known locally as "Wa Bio", is also a significant feature of the culture in the more remote parts of the island where the whole family takes part in the make-shift production. Forty-five-gallon oil drums are converted into stills, with each "still" producing as many as 1,400 bottles a year, and, apparently, the results aren't bad.

DOMINICAN REPUBLIC

Several distilleries here make rum and while some of the production is exported, these rums (Barceló and Bermúdez, for example) aren't widely known. This sugar-rich country also exports molasses.

GRENADA

Southernmost of the Windward Islands, this small "Spice Island", most famous for its nutmeg, is also planted with plenty of sugar cane. As a result, there's a thriving rum industry here with a history spanning 200 years.

The styles produced depend on the varying nature of the raw materials and the type of still used. Anything goes and there's no strong tradition for making it this way or that. Rum is also imported from elsewhere for blending and bottling.

GUADELOUPE

This is the butterfly-shaped island of the French West Indies and one of widely contrasting landscapes. Basse-Terre is the very hilly wing, not to mention the active volcano, dense with

Below
Slaves opening up the land for planting sugar cane.

rain forest, while Grande-Terre is utterly flat. It is at Grande-Terre that the sugar cane grows, introduced in 1630.

Nine distilleries make *rhums agricoles* (those made from fresh cane juice), though a fair amount of molasses-based *rhums industriels* are made too. Both are exported in bulk to other Caribbean islands and Europe (especially France). Appellation Contrôlée status guarantees origin and minimum production standards.

Just for the record, after the end of the Seven Years War in 1763, the British offered France the whole of Canada in exchange for Guadeloupe. The French refused.

HAITI

This was the first Caribbean island to which Columbus introduced sugar cane, and though it's still grown in all parts of the island, it is in the north that the best cane for rum-making is found.

Haiti freed itself from France in 1804, yet traditions and attitudes here are still predominantly French. Even today, Haitian rum continues to be made in the same way as Cognac and demand outstrips supply. Most is exported (the USA is the principal market).

JAMAICA

No centre of rum-making has been affected so much by changing tastes as Jamaica. Traditionally the source of full-bodied, slow-fermented, dark rums strengthened with dunder, the current vogue for lightness has not gone unnoticed and modern styles are much lighter, though they still lean towards the flavoursome end of the taste scale.

Rum used to be made in over 148 distilleries, 88 per cent of which belonged to the sugar mills, but production fell into decline when the sugar industry was hit badly by the developing sugar beet industry elsewhere. As a result, only a handful of rum producers survived. They all, however, make first-class rums with healthy export markets.

MARIE GALANTE

Discovered by Columbus in 1493, Marie Galante has always been an island of cane and, during the last century, the landscape was studded with no fewer than 106 windmills that drove the presses that crushed the cane that made the sugar – amazing for such a tiny dot in the ocean.

A devastating cyclone in 1928 literally ripped off the top of the last remaining windmill – a true wind of change indeed, for powerful, steam-driven factories were built to process the sugar instead, leaving the "*sucrotes*" (small sugar factories) with nothing else to do but produce rum. Even today, the majority of the cane is processed into sugar for export. The remainder (around 5 per cent) is turned into *rhum agricole*, some of which is exported.

MARTINIQUE

This French "flower island", with its mountainous rain forest and narrow valleys lined with fertile volcanic soils, has a reputation for rich, pungent rums with good ageing potential. Virtually all production is made from fresh cane juice and much is exported to France and other destinations. Appellation Contrôlée status guarantees origin and minimum production standards.

Rum production here dates back to the mid-17th century when Flemish settlers, evicted from Brazil by the Portuguese, began to disperse throughout the eastern Caribbean. They brought with them sugar cane cuttings and, most importantly, rum-making know-how, and their efforts were further advanced by French Dominican priest and alchemist Père Labat.

The sugar industry in Martinique has gone through good times and bad but sugar cane remains a significant crop here, though much has to be imported to meet the demands of the distilleries, of which there are plenty. Bacardi is also made here.

Opposite
A 1950s American ad. for Puerto Rican Bacardi. Puerto Rico now holds a near monopoly on rum imported by mainland USA.

PUERTO RICO

Home to the "cathedral of rum", the world's largest distillery owned by Bacardi, Puerto Rico has long been a vital source of rums for mainland USA. Today, 80 per cent plus of all rum consumed in the USA is Puerto Rican.

When sales started to fall after the Second

SEÑOR, ONLY BACARDI HAS IT

THAT GLAMOROUS TASTINESS
THAT MAKES A DRINK
SING

From many a swanky pantry these days come trays laden with refreshing music to the palate. It hasn't taken long for folks to sense the pleasant opportunities that lie in Bacardi . . . Cocktails, highball. Collins — each of these assumes new, appetizing glamor when it's Bacardi they're made of. Bacardi is perfectly at home in *any* drink. Once you have tried this idea—search as you may, you cannot find a satisfying substitute for true Bacardi. That secret has remained for seventy years and more within the walls of the Bacardi distilleries. *Only* Bacardi has that glamorous tastiness that makes a drink *sing*.

Copyright 1936, Schenley Import Corp., New York

ONLY *BACARDI* MAKES
BACARDI
RUM—89 PROOF

NO IMITATION CAN ACHIEVE ITS FLAVOR

World War, the US government took action. The Mature Spirits Act (1948) set out stricter standards for production, ageing and blending, improving the image and quality of the island's rums. For example, a minimum ageing period of one year is now legally required and no neutral spirits or other products can be included in the blend.

ST KITTS

Historical accounts suggest that the first French settlers here found sugar cane growing wild when they landed in 1680. True or not, sugar production, which is in the hands of the state-owned Sugar Manufacturing Company, is still an important part of the agricultural sector.

Apart from CSR, no rum is officially made here. Note the "official", since plenty of illicit rum ("culture") made from fresh sugar cane juice or syrup is consumed on St Kitts.

ST LUCIA

Some rum is made by St Lucia Distilleries under Bounty, Buccaneer, Denros, Le Marquis and Ron d'Oro labels, but only a trickle ends up overseas.

SAINT MARTIN/SINT MAARTEN

This half-French, half-Dutch island changed hands some 16 times between 1631 and 1810. One particular claim to fame is that Peter Stuyvesant (the chap who surrendered New

Amsterdam – now New York – to the British in
1664) lost his wooden leg here during a battle
with the Portuguese.

In the 1970s, this island became a leading
Caribbean holiday destination thanks to its free
port status. This, however, had a negative effect
on locally produced rums made from imported
molasses. Pott Distillery, for example, the last
operating distiller and huge exporter of bulk rums
to Germany, was forced to close down in the face
of stiff competition from cheaper imported rums
blended and bottled on the island. There is also a
thriving trade in spiced and fruit-flavoured rums.

St Vincent and The Grenadines

The supply of local molasses for the rum industry
here has always been dependent on which crop –
sugar cane or bananas – is the most profitable at
any given time. At the time of going to press,
molasses is imported here from Guyana.

Trinidad

When the British captured Trinidad from the
Spanish in 1797, molasses-based rum was already
being made. Today, Trinidad is still one of the
major sugar-producing countries of the
Caribbean and rum manufacture plays an
important role in its economy.

Plenty of rum is bottled on the island under
various labels but more is shipped around the
world in bulk. Apart from Bacardi, who have a

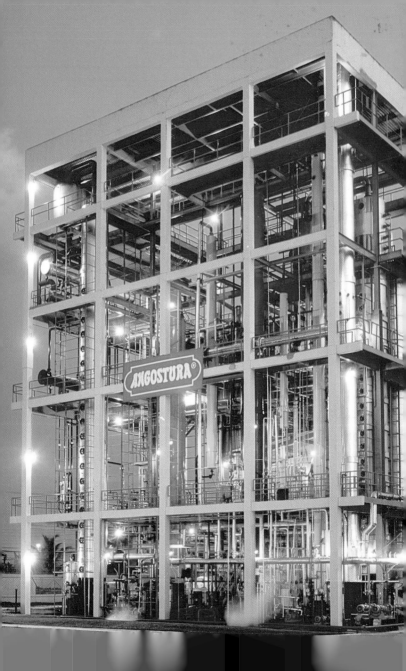

manufacturing and bottling facility here, Angostura is the principal company.

Opposite
The state-of-the-art Angostura distillery in Trinidad.

US VIRGIN ISLANDS

St Croix, St John and St Thomas are just three of the 50 islands Columbus discovered on his second voyage. They soon became the favourite haunts of pirates and Blackbeard is said to have buried his treasure here.

In the centuries that followed, the islands were ruled by the English, Dutch, Spanish, French, Knights of Malta and Danes. The USA bought the islands from the Danes in the First World War for 25 million dollars in gold and, nowadays, they are a playground for Americans.

Molasses production dates from the 1650s, though most of it was shipped to New England at first. Declaration of free port status in the early 18th century, however, made it more profitable to turn it into rum that became the linchpin of the economy. Even today, rum is one of USVI's biggest exports, though the molasses used to make it is now imported.

NORTH AMERICA

BERMUDA

Famous for Gosling's Black Seal.

CANADA

I've yet to visit a Canadian liquor store that doesn't dedicate a lot of shelf space to rum – it's the second most popular spirits segment after rye whiskey.

Canada has a long tradition of rum-making, dating back to the mid-18th century and, today, various rums are made or blended by regional distilleries for local markets. Bacardi is manufactured, too, and many other international brands are also blended and bottled here. Canada's greatest prize, however, is Seagram who own a number of "classic" labels, most notably Captain Morgan, the world's second-bestselling rum brand.

UNITED STATES

Rum production began in New England from molasses supplied by West Indian planters. Its success was instantaneous and rum became New England's largest and most profitable industry. Its importance faded, however, with the change in public preference to whiskey.

Today, the USA is the second-largest consumer of rum in the world after the Philippines. A number of facilities make rum from local sugar cane molasses, although very few find their way on to international markets. Others blend and bottle imported rums (particularly those from Puerto Rico and the US Virgin Islands). Some of the international brands are also bottled here (Bacardi and Cockspur, for instance).

CENTRAL AMERICA

BELIZE
A tiny amount of rum is produced here for local drinking.

GUATEMALA
A small amount of molasses-based rum is produced here. Most is drunk locally but some is exported to the USA and elsewhere.

HONDURAS
Known for Flor de Caña production only.

Above
A West Indian sugar mill in the early 1800s.

Opposite
Bacardi girls
shaking up
something tropical.
Mexico is now
Bacardi's number
one market.

MEXICO

Hernando Cortés introduced sugar cane to "New Spain" in 1519 but it wasn't until the 1930s that rum production took off on any truly commercial scale. A surprising amount is now made thanks to Bacardi and Seagram. Both have large-volume plants here where production is geared mainly towards the export market, either in its finished form or as raw distillate. Bacardi's Mexican distillery was the first to be opened by the company outside Cuba and is still one of their primary production facilities. One of the largest consumers of rum in Latin America, Mexico is Bacardi's number one market.

NICARAGUA

All styles are made here, though the best-known tend to be light-bodied and very dry. Production is dominated by Compañia Licorare de Nicaragua (Flor de Caña).

PANAMA

The only rum of importance is Bacardi which is manufactured here.

SOUTH AMERICA

ARGENTINA

Tiny amounts of rum are produced here with some exports to other South American countries. Far more important is Argentina's role as a supplier of raw molasses to the Caribbean.

BOLIVIA

At least one sugar producer here also distils rum, marketed domestically and exported to neighbouring countries in bottle.

BRAZIL

Brazil has one of the highest levels of spirits' consumption in Latin America dominated by cachaça, exported in modest but growing quantities. Brazil is also home to one of Bacardi's manufacturing facilities.

COLOMBIA

Rum is made in fairly large volume and some – Oro Añejo Reserva and Viejo De Caldas, for example – is of premium quality. Exports, however, are minimal.

ECUADOR

At least five distilleries produce rum of various styles for the local market.

Opposite

Sailors receiving their daily rum ration c. 1900 – demerara rum from Guyana was the preferred "grog" of the Royal Navy.

GUYANA

Hugely important former British colony closely identified with Demerara county, named after the river that irrigates the sugar cane plantations. During the 18th and 19th centuries, Demerara rum was the principal product used by the Royal Navy for its rum ration and, as a result, has achieved distinction in several parts of the world.

Today, most of the large blenders and bottlers of rum in the UK and Canada use Demerara rum as the basis of their brands. Guyana is also a considerable source of molasses for those Caribbean islands that do not cultivate sugar.

PERU
Sugar cane was first planted here in 1533 but rum production didn't begin until 1929. Destileria Peruana was the first to achieve this and remains the country's major rum manufacturer.

SURINAM
Aged and unaged rums are produced here for local consumption.

URUGUAY
ANCAP is the state refinery manufacturing petrol, oil, alcohol, cement…and rum. Domestic sales only.

VENEZUELA
Geography plants Venezuela firmly in South America but this country possesses a massive Caribbean coastline and the Caribbean influence is very much in evidence: Venezuela ranks as one of the largest consumers of rum in Latin America and is home to the second-largest rum producer in the world, Industrias Pampero. More and more top-notch Venezuelan rum is finding its way on to foreign shelves.

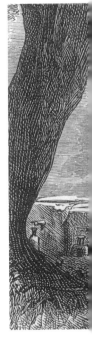

AFRICA

GHANA
Tiny production for the domestic market only.

KENYA
Lamb's Navy and Lamb's White under licence plus local brands.

MADAGASCAR
There's plenty of rum around here – everything from overproof white to aged dark. Some of it is blended from island-produced spirits; others are blends of imported rums. Domestic market only.

Malawi
Local rum only.

South Africa
"Umhali Water", as rum was first known here, was advertised for sale as early as 1861. This two-year-old, molasses-based rum was described as "equal to the Finest Jamaica". However, others were less scrupulous about the quality of their distillate and, to avoid prohibitive excise duties, very rough "Gavine" soon found its way on to the

Above
Distilling spirit from sugar cane, Madagascar, late 19th century.

black market. "Rum shops" popped up everywhere, supplied with overproof spirit in four-gallon jars by small local distilleries – you simply turned up with your empty bottle or stayed to have a tot. Interestingly, by law this spirit was not allowed to be described as rum and was called cane spirit instead. Only the imported variety was known as rum.

Most modern brands are made from blends of cane spirit purchased from a number of distilleries around the country who, unless they have their own sugar plantations, buy their molasses from various sugar mills.

ZIMBABWE
Some rum is imported for blending with local spirit. Domestic consumption.

INDIAN OCEAN

MAURITIUS

Opposite
Sampling the
final product in
a cane field,
Mauritius.

Sugar cane was first cultivated by the Dutch in 1650 and, today, it accounts for no less than 93 per cent of the total cultivated area. It's not surprising, therefore, that rum is made too. The first sugar factory-cum-distillery was built in 1740, 25 years after administration had been transferred from the Dutch to the French East India Company. Though sugar-making virtually collapsed in 1759, a thirst for cane spirit remained. Indeed, by 1772, the 125 licensed taverns in Port Louis were nothing more than

"rum shops". Local consumption dropped dramatically when the island became British in 1810, although Britain was certainly one of the countries to which the excess was exported.

Today, most production is *rhum agricole* consumed locally, though some is exported to France or made under licence for the South Africa market.

RÉUNION
Most Réunion rums are white but a small quantity of rich, dark and fruity cask-matured rums is also produced.

ASIA & THE EAST INDIES
INDIA
A relatively young industry (1950s), the majority of Indian rum is produced (by 121 distillers) for the Indian Armed Forces who consume it in vast quantities. It's a country to watch, however, and some exports are already on the world scene.

INDONESIA
Java makes Batavia Arak from local sugar cane – very dry, light-bodied and exceedingly fragrant, and very popular in Sweden where it's sweetened,

flavoured and compounded into a liqueur called Arrack Punch or Caloric Punsch.

PHILIPPINES

Rich soil and an ideal balance of sunshine and rain combine to nurture some of the finest sugar cane in the world. Following his purchase of the Calatagan Estate in 1837, one of the very first planters, Domingo Roxas, became a pioneer in the manufacture of rum. But not before he and a

Above
Even today, small producers in India rely on more traditional means of bringing the harvest home.

Below

The Philippines, currently, the world's top rum drinking country, once banned the sale of rum in the late 19th century. The spirit had to be sneaked past port authorities in small casks rather than the typical great barrels such as the one shown here.

fellow producer had fought a protracted battle with the government of the time who held the monopoly on rum production that protected revenue from sales of imported Spanish wine and Spanish brandy (the islands were under Spanish rule at this time).

With the removal of these restrictions, Roxas was able to proceed with his plans to build a distillery. In 1854 Elizalde & Company Inc. was

established, and it became the parent of the Tanduay Distillery, a notable modern-day survivor.

Filipinos enjoy over 3.5 million cases of rum each year – 85 per cent of it dark or gold. But rum has also been exported to the US since before the Second World War, still the most significant export destination. There's a touch of irony here since back in the late 18th century, when the first American ships docked in Manila, the cargomasters had great trouble disposing of their rum loads thanks to a law banning its sale "because of the effects that drunkenness had on the natives". (They soon learned to bring it in small casks so that they could pass it off as Spanish brandy.)

"Basi", made from cane juice, bark and berries, is another traditional local drink, infamous for being so "difficult and tedious" to make. First the cane must be cut on a clear moonlit night. Then the juice is poured into big iron kettles that are heated over a slow fire – the flavours aren't added until the juice starts to foam. After that it's decanted into demijohns that are buried underground for at least three years. It's probably simplest to stick to the rum – which is very good!

AUSTRALASIA

AUSTRALIA

When sugar cane was first introduced to the rich volcanic soils of Queensland in 1864, dozens of mills were built to process the sugar and, by the end of the century, at least thirteen of them were also making rum (interestingly, old stock books show that some of this early production was exported to Scotland). It tended to be favoured in the outback because, unlike beer, it didn't turn sour in the heat and needed no refrigeration.

Nowadays, rum is something of an unsung hero in Australia, yet it's the second drink to beer. Locally bottled Bacardi steals a huge share of the market but Australia's home-produced rums are incredibly popular, too – indeed, Bundaberg outsells Johnnie Walker (the world's bestselling Scotch whisky) by two to one and is the bestselling brand in Australia with an expanding reputation abroad.

NEW ZEALAND
Very few indigenous rums.

EUROPE – A SPECIAL CASE
Aside from Bacardi's manufacturing facility in Spain, relatively minuscule amounts of rum are distilled here. Nevertheless rum-drinking is ingrained in the European consciousness, especially in countries that have, or

Right
Columbus
arriving in Cuba.
Europeans
provided the
original
technology for
distilling in the
Caribbean and
still prefer to
import rum from
the region rather
than distilling it
themselves.

used to have, overseas Caribbean territories. The French, for example, drink vast quantities of rum from Martinique, Guadeloupe, Marie Galante and Réunion that are often matured, blended and bottled in Le Havre or Bordeaux and sold under various labels.

In the 1960s, Germany was the second-largest rum market in the world. Two leading blenders and bottlers (Pott and Hansen) decided to set up manufacturing plants in the Dutch Antilles as a result, but these were not successful and German rum consumption has been slipping ever since. Nevertheless, the Germans still drink more rum than the French and British, and even the Brazilians! Apart from *Echter Rum* ("true" rum), they enjoy a style known as "*Rum Verschnitt*" that is made of concentrated Jamaican rum mixed with 95 per cent neutral grain spirit. This kind of rum is known as "*Inländer Rum*" in Austria where it's also a favourite.

There are also hundreds of very popular rums on sale in Eastern Europe, particularly in the Czech Republic and Slovakia. Distilled locally, many of these are flavoured or spiced and some even rely on rum essence for taste. Wherever you go here, however, you can buy sweetened hot rum punch, the local speciality. And its name? '*Grog*'.

Postscript: the UK

The UK boasts a long, colourful and unique rum history. Many brands sold worldwide are aged, blended, bottled and brokered here while others are put together exclusively for domestic sales.

Barbados, Guyana, Jamaica and Trinidad continue to be of vital importance to the British rum trade, dating from the days when each distillery would import its own individual rum mark from the sugar plantations that crowded these former British colonies. As demand increased, it became more economical to import rum in bulk and the benefits of ageing the rum in a damp and cool climate soon became obvious. Membership of the EU has altered the pattern of trade but Britain's reputation for fine blends still holds true today.

Odd though it may seem, there's historical evidence that rum was actually *distilled* here. The product of the Scottish Leith and Glasgow's sugar refineries was "scarce to be discerned or known from the finest of the foreign brandy" according to its manufacturers in 1684. Punters who had to drink it disagreed, however, describing it as "plague water", although it was probably no less crude than the West Indian rum of that time.

There's plenty of
Old St. Croix at your
favorite store

CHAPTER FIVE

A–Z OF CLASSIC BRANDS AND THEIR PRODUCERS

When I first set about compiling this chapter, I found that I'd "collected" over 2,700 different labels, which left me with the difficult task of deciding which brands to write about.

Many rums are produced by the "big boys" on an international scale while others, often teased out of tiny distilleries, never pass the lips of anyone but the "locals" or tourists seeking interesting olfactory and gustatory diversions. The latter can be intriguing but are hardly "classic", so for the purposes of this A–Z I have concentrated on producers who have an export (or re-export) market for their brands. I've also virtually ignored the vast array of spiced and flavoured rums. Not surprisingly Caribbean rums dominate the resulting list, but there are some eye-opening exceptions.

The brand/producer name is given first. The country in brackets refers to the country of distillation even if the molasses/cane juice is not indigenous and/or ageing and blending takes place elsewhere. Strength can vary depending on country of sale.

Opposite

St Croix in the US Virgin Islands, home to Blackbeard's buried treasure, so they say, provides the image for this old brand of rum.

ANGOSTURA Trinidad

Producer of the famous bitters but also makes 94 per cent of all rum consumed in Trinidad and Tobago via wholly owned subsidiaries Trinidad Distillers Ltd and Fernandes Distillers Ltd.

The Angostura story started with Dr J.G.B. Siegart, Surgeon General of the military hospital in Venezuela under General Simón Bolívar. He developed a mixture of tropical herbs, spices and alcohol for use as a medicinal tonic that took its name from the town on the Orinoco river where Bolívar was headquartered.

A thriving business was established, moved to Trinidad and, in 1936, began manufacturing its own alcohol under the direction of Siegart's grandson. It was but a small step from here to make a variety of molasses-based, column-distilled rums.

Apart from producing rums for their own brands, aged rums are bulk-sold to blenders on other Caribbean islands. Angostura also supplies raw rum in bulk to other blenders in over 140 countries.

See also Fernandes, Old Oak, Royal Oak, Trinidad Distillers

ANTIGUA DISTILLERY
Founded in 1932, Antigua distillery introduced the first continuous still to the island, revolutionising the rum industry. Uses Guyanan molasses and all ageing is done in charred, 220-litre, ex-Bourbon, oak casks. Exports to other Caribbean islands (often in bulk), Europe and the USA.

CAVALIER
Five labels - Dark and Light, both two years old at 43 per cent abv; dark-coloured five year old (43 per cent abv); and Light and Dark 151 Overproof (75.5 per cent abv). Export volumes exceed local sales.

ENGLISH HARBOUR (40 per cent abv)
White aged for two to three years. Also six-year-old and 16-year-old golden blends plus 151 white (75.5 per cent abv).

APPLETON ESTATE Jamaica
Jamaica's best-known rum, exported to over 60 countries (Mexico is the number one market). Owned by J. Wray & Nephew, Appleton Estate has been a rum-producing sugar plantation since at least the 1740s and its 3,700 acres of sugar cane fields occupy most of the fertile Nassau Valley. Indeed, the estate provides roughly two-thirds of Wray & Nephew's cane sugar needs, the balance coming from local farmers. The sugar factory can

produce up to 160 tons of sugar per day and the distillery has a production capacity of ten million litres of rum per annum.

APPLETON ESTATE WHITE
(37.5, 40 and 43 per cent abv)
Product of the continuous still but given a lovely, subtle, delicate flavour from two and a half years in oak (considerably longer than most whites). Easy-going, light, fruity flavours with hints of bananas and sweet oils.

Appleton Special
(40 and 43 per cent abv)
Whisky was scarce during the Second World War and experiments were carried out at Appleton Estate to produce a rum that would serve as a substitute. The result was "Appleton Estate Special", renamed "Appleton Special" in the mid-1990s. Golden rum, hand-blended from full-flavoured, aged, pot-still rums with a dash of lighter column-still rums. Full, honey-rich nose but mild and smooth to taste in a light to medium-bodied style.

Appleton Estate Dark
(38 and 40 per cent abv)
Full-flavoured, oak-aged blend with hints of almonds and spiced apples.

Appleton Estate 12-Year-Old
(43 per cent abv)
Blend of very smooth, fine rums comparable to the finest old Cognac – and drunk in the same way. Wonderful mahogany hue with peat and exotic fruits on the nose with echoes of eucalyptus and dried berries. Bold in character with a smooth, rich, herbal sweetness to taste and a complex finish.

APPLETON ESTATE 21-YEAR-OLD
(43 per cent abv)
J. Wray & Nephew's premium rum. Mature, mellow rums are hand-blended and then aged for a further two years. Deep mahogany colour. Light, delicate bouquet. Robust yet medium-bodied flavours. A powerful yet delicate rum with remarkable finesse.

APPLETON ESTATE V/X
(40 and 43 per cent abv)
Hugely popular, 'very exceptional', full-flavoured golden blend of several marks of rums aged separately in small barrels for a minimum of five years. Seductively rich aromas of brown sugar, citrus and spice preface a broody, intense, subtly sweet taste. Well-balanced with a satiny texture and a delightfully firm and toasty finish.

See also J. Wray & Nephew

BACARDI-MARTINI

Family-owned through six generations, Bacardi not only boasts the world's best-selling spirit brand (over 20 million cases a year) but, on acquiring Martini & Rossi in 1992, consolidated its position as one of the top five global spirit-producing companies – "Bacardi" is a name instantly recognisable in 175 countries. Not bad for a company that started life in a tin shack!

It all began with Spanish wine merchant Don Facundo Bacardi y Maso who emigrated to Santiago de Cuba in 1830. Rum was a rough and raw, dark and fiery drink then and he soon set about experimenting with ways to improve it. In 1862, having bought a small distillery with his sons, Don Facundo not only released the world's first white rum but also a spirit that was completely new in taste. Bacardi quickly became

Below

The original Bacardi premises which the family were forced to leave behind following Castro's revolution.

CUNA DEL " BACARDI "ESTABLECIDOS 1862
SANTIAGO DE CUBA

the most popular rum in Cuba and, by the turn of the century, was renowned in all the world's great capitals.

Overseas operations began in 1910 when Bacardi was bottled in Spain. This was followed by the opening of a manufacturing plant in Mexico in the 1930s – an expansionist step unprecedented by any other spirit maker, and a cunning way of minimising the punitive import duties that rendered Bacardi less competitive in certain markets. In 1936, for example, Bacardi began to make rum in Puerto Rico. Domestic status allowed Bacardi to grab a share of the American rum market and provided a legitimate way of avoiding the $1.00 per bottle tax imposed on imports at the time. That this strategy worked was borne out by the figures – by the early 1940s, revenue from Bacardi made outside Cuba exceeded that from rum made "at home".

In the wake of the 1960 Cuban revolution, company assets worth over $76 million were seized illegally. Having had the foresight to transfer the Bacardi trademarks in 1958, however, the company survived the debacle of counterfeit Bacardi being produced in their confiscated Cuban facilities.

Bacardi now controls a stunning empire: primary production facilities are located in Mexico and Puerto Rico, but it is also manufactured in the Bahamas, Brazil, Canada, Martinique, Panama, Spain and Trinidad (with

Opposite
This Prohibition era postcard depicting Uncle Sam being flown to Cuba by a Bacardi bat was given to American tourists in Havana to send back to the USA.

FLYING TO HEAVEN
WITH BACARDI

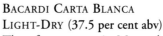

Above
The evolution of
the Bacardi logo.

plans for a facility in China). In addition, Bacardi is bottled in Australia, Austria, France, Germany, New Zealand, Switzerland, the UK and the USA. Amazingly, there's a uniformity of quality of Bacardi rum wherever it is made.

The bat was adopted as the company's logo very early on when most consumers were unable to read. Legend has it that Don Facundo's wife suggested this as a symbol of good luck and family unity.

BACARDI CARTA BLANCA LIGHT-DRY (37.5 per cent abv)

The famous one! Matured in uncharred white oak barrels for one year, filtered before and after ageing, it's white and dry with a slightly candied nose and minerally, peppery finish. Every batch is certified in Bacardi's high-tech laboratories in Nassau and has to pass a blind tasting test before being offered for sale, regardless of its origin. Most of us drink it with cola but it's surprisingly enjoyable on the rocks or with tonic.

BACARDI EXCLUSIV (40 per cent abv)
Premium, quadruple-distilled white introduced in selected US markets in early 1998. Described as the first ultra-filtered rum giving exceptional purity while retaining flavour.

**BACARDI CARTA DE ORO
(37.5 to 40 per cent abv)**
Starts as the same blend of light spirits as Carta Blanca, but aged for up to two years in charred oak and not refiltered after ageing. Full body with a nutty, vanilla nose, some nut and spice flavours and a dry, buttery finish.

**BACARDI 151 OVERPROOF
(75.5 per cent abv)**
Premium gold designed to give an extra kick to rum-based cocktails.

**BACARDI AÑEJO
(40 per cent abv)**
Six-year-old blend of golden rums. Clean, bright and well balanced with light body. Some spiciness with citrus and oak flavours.
BACARDI RESERVE (40 per cent abv)

Golden blend of rums up to six years old, sporting apricot, peach and banana aromas and a light, fruity flavour tinged with maple syrup.

BACARDI 8 (40 per cent abv)

Niche, top-of-the-range, amber blend of super-premium rums aged in mature white American oak for eight years and, until 1997, traditionally reserved for the Bacardi family. Based on the original "recipe" created by Don Facundo Bacardi, it has a wonderfully complex nose of apricots, vanilla and nutmeg with smooth, rich, spice and oak flavours, complemented by a deliciously sweet finish. Limited production.

BACARDI PREMIUM BLACK (40 per cent abv)

Labelled as Bacardi Select in the USA. Some of the constituent rums in the blend are aged for four years in charred barrels. This gives most of the colour which is then adjusted with caramel. Despite the ebony colour, it's clearly differentiated from other dark rums, delivering quite a light body with a sweet molasses nose, candied flavours and an aftertaste of black coffee.

BACARDI 1873 SOLERA (40 per cent abv)
Spice, apple and burnt sugar flavours abound, but slightly less pronounced than those of Bacardi Black.

BACARDI SPICE (40 per cent abv)
Introduced in 1996, this blend of premium dark Bacardi rums and Caribbean spices has recently been remixed and is now aged in oak for two years. To taste, it's now softer and creamier.

**BACARDI LIMÓN
(35 per cent abv)**
Sweet blend of Carta Blanca, natural lemon and lemon extract. Shattered the company's record for first-year sales, selling more than 350,000 cases in the first nine months.

See also Castillo, Trinidad Distillers

BARBANCOURT Haiti
Haiti's signature rum. The distillery was built in 1862 by Frenchman Dupré Barbancourt who applied his knowledge of cognac to the rum-making process.

A three-day fermentation of the juice of locally grown cane (30 per cent directly cultivated by the company) is distilled by the charentaise method – wash is twice-distilled in a copper pot still to give a 90 per cent abv distillate that is watered down to 50 per cent abv with filtered rainwater before being vatted in Limousin oak. All Barbancourt rums are aged before bottling which, in turn, always takes place at the distillery.

Below

Barbancourt rums... made in the some way as fine cognac.

The double-distillation and high original strength make a unique style of amber-coloured *rhums agricoles* – vanilla-scented and full-bodied with lush, velvety-sweet, slightly spicy flavours hinting nutmeg and cocoa and a long, dry finish reminiscent of cognac. Production volumes are low (demand always outstrips supply – indeed, Barbancourt rums are only available in Haitian stores in November) but quality is revered.

Three styles: versatile, four-year-old Three Star; premium, eight-year-old Five Star Réserve Spéciale; super-premium Estate Réserve du Domaine, a limited release, 15-year-old blend selected from private family reserves. All are bottled at either 40 or 43 per cent abv.

Export destinations include Belgium, Canada, Ecuador, Germany, Italy, Panama, Spain and Sint Maarten. The USA is the chief export market, although the 1991-4 Haiti-US embargo almost killed off business.

BARCELÓ Dominican Republic

Good quality, molasses-based, column-distilled rums produced mainly for the domestic market. Four styles: Blanco (40 per cent abv); Añejo (up to three years old, 40 per cent abv); Gran Añejo (up to four years old, 40 per cent abv); and premium Imperial (six years old, 38 per cent abv).

BARDINET France

Bordeaux-based owner and distributor of certain *rhums agricoles* brands.

See also DePaz, Dillon, Montebello

BERMÚDEZ Dominican Republic

Premium, molasses-based, column-distilled rums that are unusual in that they're aged in used oak barrels from England at only 50 per cent abv. This gives very good flavours of dried orange peel and butterscotch with lovely sweet edges which are heightened with age. In spite of their obvious quality, these rums are quite hard to find outside the Caribbean, parts of Central and South America, Italy and Spain.

BLACK FORT XXX India
(42.8 per cent abv)
From Som Distilleries, one of the most modern spirit-producing facilities in India. Black Fort XXX is exported to Hong Kong, the Middle East, Netherlands, Russia, Taiwan and the UK.

BRUGAL Dominican Republic

Good, molasses-based, column-distilled rums sold locally and in the USA. Three labels: White (aged three years; 43 per cent abv); tropical fruit-flavoured Gold (aged three years; 43 per cent abv); Añejo (aged three years plus; 43 per cent abv). The latter is the most interesting - an upmarket, after-dinner style steeped in aromas of butter, oak, hazelnuts and toffee with semi-sweet, multi-layered flavours of butterscotch, honey and dark chocolate.

BUNDABERG Australia

The Queensland town of Bundaberg was central to Australia's booming sugar industry during the 1880s and, by 1888, the Bundaberg distillery had been established. Until the 1950s, the company

only sold their rum in cask to fellow Australians for own-labels. Since then, however, and despite having burned down twice – "not due to overzealous barbies" – the "Bundy" name has spread across the world. Exports aside, Bundaberg "genuine, down-to-earth and no bullshit" rum is the biggest-selling Australian spirit brand in its homeland, dominating the dark rum category with a 90 per cent share.

Molasses ("black gold") is supplied by the Millaquin sugar mill and the fermented wash is double-distilled, first in a single-column still, then in a pot still. Two years ageing in 60,000-litre white American oak vats (there are 150 of these,

Above
A Queensland sugar mill.

each made of six tons of timber) gives a full, rich and distinctively tasty drink of 37 per cent abv. The reddish colour comes from adding caramel halfway through maturation.

A limited edition of Bundaberg Black was released in 1995 from a specially selected vat of exceptionally smooth and mellow rum, set aside in 1986. As no two vats age in the same way,

future editions will be different yet again.

The polar bear logo symbolises that Bundaberg keeps out the "wickedest cold".

CACIQUE Venezuela

World's sixth largest seller from Licorerias Unidas (now Seagram-owned). Distils, ages and bottles more than 3.5 million cases of molasses-based rum a year, mainly under this label.

Prime raw materials and a careful production process combining traditional methods and state-of-the-art technology give excellent quality. Export markets include Bolivia, Canada, the Canary Islands, Chile, Ecuador, Germany, Italy, Mexico, Peru, Portugal and Spain.

Three labels: Silver (premium white; 40 per cent abv); Añejo (golden blend of seven different aged rums of three different distillation systems; first bottled in 1961; 40 per cent abv); Añejo 500 (luxury sipping version; aged two to eight years; 40 per cent abv).

See also Seagram

CADENHEAD'S UK

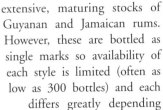

Scottish importer, established 1842, holding extensive, maturing stocks of Guyanan and Jamaican rums. However, these are bottled as single marks so availability of each style is limited (often as low as 300 bottles) and each differs greatly depending on cask size and exact storage conditions. Expanding worldwide sales mean that whereas bottling used to take place every two years or so, they now bottle every nine months to meet demand.

FROM GUYANA:

DATED DISTILLATION DEMERARA
32-YEAR-OLD (72.1 per cent abv)
Pot-still rum from Demerara Distillers' Uitvlugt Distillery. Bonded 1964. Bottled at natural cask strength June 1997. Slightly smoky nose with very smooth, dry flavours and lingering finish.

DATED DISTILLATION DEMERARA
35-YEAR-OLD (Cask Strength)
Column-distilled rum from Enmore Distillery, bottled spring 1998.

Green Label Demerara Ten-Year-Old
(46 per cent abv)
Perfumed, spearmint nose with a very light smoky tinge.

Green Label Demerara 24-Year-Old
(46 per cent abv)
Fresh, floral and woody nose with a soft, dry, rich, smoky-syrup flavour with traces of coffee. Pot-still rum aged in American oak.

Green Label Demerara 25-Year-Old
(46 per cent abv)
Bottled spring 1998.

Green Label Nine-Year-Old
(46 per cent abv)
Lightly scented nose with traces of marzipan. Marzipan again on taste with an almost minty freshness and warming aniseed glow. Pot-still rum.

Green Label 25-Year-Old
(46 per cent abv)
Bottled spring 1998. Pot-still rum.

FROM JAMAICA:

DATED DISTILLATION TEN-YEAR-OLD
(75 per cent abv)
Column-distilled, heavy-bodied wedderburn rum
(see Chapter 3) bonded 1986; bottled at cask strength
October 1997. Light, fragrant, fresh fruit salad nose
with tropical sweetness and long, warm finish.

DATED DISTILLATION 22-YEAR-OLD
(68.9 per cent abv)
Column-distilled rum from Long
Pond Estate. Sweet, rich flavours akin
to black treacle with hints of spearmint.

GREEN LABEL TEN-YEAR-OLD
(46 per cent abv)
Most popular of Cadenhead rums,
made from column-distilled
wedderburn rum (see Chapter 3),
aged in barrels from Long Pond
Estate. Coconuts and charred
wood bouquet balanced by strong
hints of butter and vanilla.

GREEN LABEL 22-YEAR-OLD
(46 per cent abv)
Orange peel nose. Sweet on tip of
tongue with a sour cream veneer.
Originates from the Frome Distillery
which closed in the year that the contents of
this cask were distilled.

CAPTAIN MORGAN

The Captain Morgan tradition started some three hundred years ago when Henry Morgan, one-time intrepid buccaneer and Governor of Jamaica, began to cultivate sugar cane on his Jamaican estates and make his famous rum. Today, it's the flagship rum in Seagram's portfolio, the second-bestselling rum brand in the world and the leading dark rum brand in the UK.

Blending and bottling takes place at various Seagram sites around the world which explains why the packaging is not entirely consistent.

Principal labels:

CAPTAIN MORGAN
BLACK LABEL
(37.5 and 40 per cent abv)
World's largest-selling dark rum. Rich and smooth with warm, fruity flavours, medium body and a lingering, sweet liquorice finish. Traditional, pot-distilled Long Pond Estate Jamaican rums, some aged up to seven years, are blended with column-distilled rums from Guyana and Barbados.

CAPTAIN MORGAN ORIGINAL SPICED
(35 per cent abv)

First of the major spiced styles to be launched and brand leader in the spiced rum category. Honey-coloured blend of rums, mellow spices and natural flavours including vanilla, apricot, fig and tincture of cassia. Has an appealing, spicy, honeyed nose and flavours of vanilla, nutmeg, coriander and cinnamon wrapped in a creamy texture. Long, tropical-fruit finish with a slight bite.

CAPTAIN MORGAN PRIVATE STOCK
(40 per cent abv)

Premium, spiced, golden style blended with spices and other natural flavours. Made at Serrallés from fine Puerto Rican rum. More mature and less aromatic than Original Spiced. Nose of sherry, coriander and nutmeg. Butterscotch sweetness complemented by an aftertaste of vanilla and cinnamon. Popular in North America.

CAPTAIN MORGAN PARROT BAY
(24 per cent abv)

Clear rum with tropical flavours and natural coconut.

See also Seagram, Serrallés

CARONI Trinidad

A true by-product of the Caroni Sugar Factory since rum production (using the leftover molasses) doesn't begin until the estate's sugar-processing season has finished. Distilled in either a pot still, or a two-column continuous still, the majority of this distinctively light and smooth rum is immediately bulk-exported to buyers in Europe, Canada and the Caribbean. However, some is kept for ageing in charred oak casks and sold under their own labels. At the time of writing, there's some question about the future of this company and the Board is said to be considering a joint venture for its rum division with Angostura Holdings.

AUTHENTIC
(43 per cent abv)
Premium export blend of estate rums. White and Gold labels, both very mellow and smooth.

WHITE MAGIC
(40 and 43 per cent abv)
Three-year-old, carbon-filtered blend, a trendsetter in light rums in Trinidad.

PUNCHEON RUM
(75 per cent abv)
Velvet-smooth, overproof white.

STALLION PUNCHEON (75 per cent abv)
Unaged white bottled for the locals and one of the strongest rums in Trinidad and Tobago. Noted for its purity and clean taste.

FÉLICITÉ GOLD (40 and 43 per cent abv)
Stylish blend of three-year-old golden rums. Distinguished by its generous fragrance, mellowness and natural lightness. First blended in 1820 from cane grown on the Félicité Estate.

SPECIAL OLD CASK (40 and 43 per cent abv)
Premium blend from a selection of fine ten-year-old rums. Mellow and soft with a silky finish.

CASTILLO Puerto Rico
Bacardi brand popular locally, in Ecuador and on mainland USA.

SILVER (40 per cent abv)
Light, dry, one-year-old white.

GOLD (40 per cent abv)
Aged for a minimum of three years.

SPICED (40 per cent abv)
Aromas of sugar candy, vanilla and tutti-frutti.

See also Bacardi

CAVALIER Antigua
See Antigua Distillery

CHARLES SIMONNET
Guadeloupe
Now-independent distillery linked, quite literally, via a series of pipes across a road to the French state-owned *sucrerie*. When built in 1928, they were one and the same enterprise. Governed by the sugar-production cycle, some of the output is *rhum agricole*, the remainder *rhum industriel*. Both are made in a unique column still arrangement designed to fit the building.

Roughly 90 per cent of the 2 million litres of rum distilled annually is shipped in bulk to France for bottling under the Simonnet label (50 and 55 per cent abv unaged white *rhum agricole;* four-year-old Rhum Vieux 45 per cent abv and unaged Fajou, a 50 per cent abv blend of *agricole* and *industriel*) or sold to other bottlers. The balance is drunk locally or shipped in bottle to other Caribbean islands.

C.J. WRAY Jamaica
(40 per cent abv)
Aged white that is seriously dry to taste – indeed, Wray & Nephew assert "nothing drier, nothing better". Lovely herbal flavour with notes of cedar, pine and smoke.

See also J. Wray & Nephew

CLÉMENT Martinique

Below
M. Homère
Clément who
acquired his
Habitation
Clément in
1887.

Established 1887 and considered by many as the aristocrat of Martinique *rhums agricoles*. Highly polished, flavoursome, sipping styles are made from free-run cane juice column-distilled in Clément's own still installed at Distillerie Simon, though maturation and bottling are carried out at the Habitation Clément.

Below M. Homère Clément who acquired his Habitation Clément in 1887.

After generous time in cask, demineralised water is used to bring it to bottle strength. Nothing strange in this *per se*. However, Clément achieves this in very small stages and the mixing is done in 34,000-litre tanks to allow plenty of oxygenation. It's time-consuming, but gives roundness and texture with none of the fieriness normally associated with new rum.

Big sales in Martinique. Exported to Belgium, Canada, other Caribbean islands, France, Italy, Japan, Mexico, Russia, Spain and Sweden.

RHUM BLANC (50 and 55 per cent abv)

Essentially unaged white rum even though it's spent a few months in wood. Distinguished by a gentle, almost floral, fragrance of sugar cane and lemon.

RHUM VIEUX SIX-YEAR-OLD (44 per cent abv)

Woody aromas with black pepper, lemon peel, dill and basil. Very concentrated syrupy-sweetness and a long, voluptuous finish.

RHUM VIEUX TEN-YEAR-OLD (44 per cent abv)

Evolved, oaky nose. Subtly sweet on the palate with flavours of sherry, butter and mint.

RHUM VIEUX 15-YEAR-OLD
(44 per cent abv)
Dried fruit, roasted hazelnut and liquorice bouquet. Complex, sweet and creamy taste and texture and a really long finish.

CUVÉE SPÉCIALE HOMÈRE CLÉMENT **(44 per cent abv)**
Aromas of dried fruit mingle with cinnamon. Elaborately oaky.

TRÈS VIEUX 1970
(44 per cent abv)
Spiritous nose of tobacco, spices and hazelnuts. Semi-sweet biscuity flavour, almost chewy in texture and a velvety, fleshy finish.

TRÈS VIEUX 1952
(44 per cent abv)
Subtle aroma of dried flowers, ripe fruits, caraway seeds and walnuts. Harmonious, oak and liquorice flavours are a prelude to an exceptionally long finish. Like an XO cognac and absolutely superb.

See also Distillerie Simon

COCKSPUR Barbados

Barbados's leading golden rum blended by Hanschell Inniss, founded by Danish sea captain Valdemar Hanschell who set up his first ship's chandlery and liquor store in 1884. Until 1973, there was always difficulty in finding adequate supply of raw spirit. This changed, however, when Hanschell Inniss became part of Goddard Enterprises who were partners in the West Indies Rum Distillery.

All blending is carried out at Hanschell Inniss's premises from where it is either bulk-shipped (aged or unaged) or bottled, depending on its ultimate destination – Canada, Germany, Japan, Sweden, the UK and the USA all bottle Cockspur locally, for example.

FIVE STAR (37.5, 40 and 43 per cent abv)
Flagship blend of two-year-old golden rums, though a filtered white is also bottled. Boasts aromas of ripe melon, bananas, brown sugar, cinnamon and hay. Medium-bodied in style with flavours of tobacco and cereal and aftertastes of honey and chocolate.

VSOR (40 and 43 per cent abv)
Top of the range "Very Special Old Reserve". Prestigious limited edition in numbered bottles. A blend of golden rums up to ten years old. Mild spice aromas and the taste of raw sugar cane, burnt sugar, spices, walnuts and dates wrapped in a soft, sweet, gentle style.

See also West Indies Rum Distillery

CORUBA DELUXE DARK PLANTER'S Jamaica
(37.2 and 40 per cent abv)
Biggest-selling spirit brand in New

Zealand, also available in the USA and Canada. Traditional, rich-flavoured, full-bodied, pot-still rum.

See also J. Wray & Nephew

CRUZAN   US Virgin Islands

Set amidst the ruins of an old plantation in Estate Diamond, St Croix, the Cruzan Rum Distillery was in the hands of the Nelthropp family until

Below
The idyllic US
Virgin Islands.

1994. Todhunter International owns it now and renamed it the Virgin Islands Rum Distillery, but the family still runs it. Uses molasses shipped from the Dominican Republic and Central and South America to make the bestselling rum brand in the US Virgin Islands. All rums are distilled in a four-column still, oak-aged for a minimum of two years and considered very clean and pure.

Eighty-five per cent of production is shipped to the USA for bottling. Some, however, say that true Cruzan rum can only be found locally owing to the quality of the "Virgin" rainwater used for bottling. Also make rum under contract for other companies.

LIGHT DRY (40 per cent abv)
Two-year-old blend.

ST CROIX PREMIUM LIGHT (40 per cent abv)
Double-distilled, two-year-old blend for the local market only.

151 GOLD (75.5 per cent abv)
Two-year-old. Light and delicate on the palate with a fairly neutral finish.

DARK DRY (40 per cent abv)
Two-year-old.

ST CROIX PREMIUM DARK (40 per cent abv)
Aged for a minimum of two years in charred oak

barrels with oak chips added. Blended for local market only.

ESTATE DIAMOND PROPRIETOR'S RESERVE
(40 per cent abv)
Cruzan's top rum, triple-distilled and a big export brand. Oak-aged four years minimum but includes 12-year-old rums. Silky smooth yet rich.

See also Todhunter

CSR St Kitts
(40 per cent abv)
"Cane Spirit Rothschild" made from juice from local cane. Demerara Distillers acquired the St Kitts Distillery and the franchise of the CSR brand name from Baron Edmond de Rothschild in 1996. Some argue that CSR breaks all the rules because it's distilled to 95 per cent abv.

See also Demerara Distillers

CUBANEY Dominican Republic
Four styles, all made from cane juice at 38 per cent abv: Cristal Reserve White three-year-old; golden Añejo Reserva five-year-old; Añejo Reserva seven-year-old; and sipping rum Tesoro Dark Ten Year Old. Distributed at home and in the Canary Islands, the Caribbean, Ecuador, Honduras and Spain. On Cubaney's launch in Cuba in 1996, Havana

Club briefly forced a ban on imports of Cubaney
– prompted, no doubt, by its overnight success.

DAMOISEAU Guadeloupe

Small, family-run business on Grande-Terre,
formerly Distillerie Bellevue. Buys unburned cane
from local farmers, hand-cut to preserve every
ounce of flavour. The fermented juice is distilled
in a single-column, stainless steel and copper still.
When sugar cane is out of season, Damoiseau
makes *rhum industriel* for bulk shipment to

France used in local labels.

Under the Damoiseau label: unaged Rhum Blanc (43, 45, 50 and 55 per cent abv); Rhum Paille (one year old; 50 per cent abv); Rhum Vieux (four, five or six years old; 45 per cent abv); Vintage (eight or 15 years old) plus a rare Vintage 1953 (45 per cent abv).

DEMERARA DISTILLERS Guyana

Demerara Distillers's reputation for producing fine rums spans 300 years. Sole producer of Demerara rums and largest bulk-supplier of Caribbean rum to brand owners in the European Community – over 7 million litres annually – plus major supplier to Canada and the USA. Produce and market their own portfolio of premium quality rums marketed internationally under the CSR and El Dorado trademarks.

Demerara Distillers sets a textbook example of quality control where tradition and modern technology rub shoulders with ease. Local sugar cane provides molasses, dunder and cane juice as raw materials. All styles of rum can be made by double-distillation in pot stills or continuous distillation in column stills – indeed, the last fully operating, rectangular, wooden Coffey Still in the Western world continues to be utilised for special rums of unique character. White American oak, ex-Bourbon casks are used for maturation.

Owns two large distilleries – Diamond (for which Seagram has world agency rights) and

Uitvlugt – plus a distillation and bottling facility on St Kitts. Bulk and bottled rums are channelled through Demerara Distillers (UK) Ltd, Demerara Rum Company, Canada and Breitenstein Produkten, Netherlands to bottlers in Europe and North America.

See also Cadenhead's, CSR, El Dorado, Seagram

DEPAZ Martinique

Opposite
Devil's inferno –
Rhum Negrita,
Dillon's brand
leader in France,
also goes by the
name Old Nick.

Estate famous for its high yields of cane, presumably because the 120 hectares of cane are planted on the slopes of Mount Pelée, rich in volcanic ash. All the cane is used for the production of four *rhums agricoles*: Rhum Blanc (unaged; 50 and 55 per cent abv); Rhum Paille (two years of maturation; 50 per cent abv); Rhum Vieux (four years old; 45 per cent abv) and Rhum Vieux Réserve Spéciale (blend of premium four-year-old rums; 45 per cent abv). Occasionally, the estate releases a special Rhum Vieux Millésime that gives the year of distillation on the label. The trademark is owned by Bardinet in France where much of DePaz rum is sold.

See also Bardinet

DILLON Martinique

Founded by Colonel Arthur Dillon in 1690, this plantation and distillery is famous for first-class,

RAGING VOLCANOES

CREATED THIS LOVELY, LIMPID RUM

In Martinique in the West Indies and Reunion in the East ... on the opposite sides of the earth ... two mountains exploded! Today the soils of these tropic islands ... rich with lava ash ... produce sugar-canes world-famous for the distilling of fine rums. And ... to bring America a new taste ... these superb rums are voyaged 10,630 nautical miles to Bordeaux, and blended. The rich full-body of the West Indies unites with the aromatic fragrance of the East to create a softer, smoother rum ... a rum unique, *distinctive* ... the incomparable RHUM NEGRITA.

RHUM NEGRITA

At your favorite bar ... TRY a

NEGRITA COLLINS

Pour jigger of RHUM NEGRITA into tall glass. Add juice of half a lemon and a spoonful of sugar. Stir, add cracked ice, and fill with soda.

oak-aged, full-bodied *rhums agricoles* made to a recipe passed down through seven generations of French and Creole families. Now owned by Bardinet, most of the production is shipped to France, though a little finds its way to the USA.

GRAND RHUM BLANC (50, 55 and 62 per cent abv)
Stored in oak for three months before bottling. The 62 per cent abv version is not exported.

RHUM PAILLE (50 per cent abv)
One year old.

NEGRITA (40 and 45 per cent abv)
Brand leader in France, imported and blended by Bardinet. To confuse things, it's also known as Old Nick or Dillon Rhum Vieux Carte Noire in Martinique itself and Dillon Dark in the USA. Aged for six years to give a very smooth, light and mellow flavour for a dark rum.

RHUM TRÈS VIEUX (45 per cent abv)
Matured for 15 years.

RHUM TRÈS VIEUX 1978 (45 per cent abv)
Spicy, aromatic nose with hints of pepper and
ginger. Very attractive depth of flavour and
weight. Gentle, after-dinner sipping style.

See also Bardinet

DISTILLERIE SIMON Martinique
No label of its own, but ferments cane juice for J.
Bally (who, in turn, distil it in their own still
which they keep here at Simon) and ferments and
distils rhums agricoles for Clément. Any ageing
and all bottling are handled by J. Bally and
Clément themselves. A further 800,000 litres of
rhum agricole is bulk-exported to France for use in
own-labels.

See also Clément, J. Bally

DON Q Puerto Rico

See Serrallés

DOORLY'S Barbados
Five styles found locally and on some export
markets: Extra Light (40 per cent abv); five-year-
old, amber Fine Old Barbados (40 and 43 per
cent abv); 151 Dark Overproof (75.5 per cent

abv); Harbour Policeman (40 per cent abv), bottled solely for the tourist market; Macaw (40, 43 and 75.5 per cent abv) which are unaged blends in White and Dark styles.

See also R.L. Seale

DUQUESNE-TROIS-RIVIÈRES
Martinique

Two separate rhum agricole brands are marketed. The largest, Trois-Rivières (unaged Rhum Blanc 40, 50 and 55 per cent abv and five-year-old Rhum Vieux 45 per cent abv), is sold mostly to the local market, while the majority of Duquesne-labelled rums are shipped to France (unaged Rhum Blanc at 50 and 55 per cent abv; ten-year-old Rhum Vieux at 45 per cent abv; and ten-year-old Rhum Vieux Spéciale VSOP, also 45 per cent abv).

Manufacture takes place at the original 600-hectare Trois-Rivières estate, founded in 1661, which can supply roughly 80 per cent of the distillery's cane sugar needs. Maturation and bottling, however, are carried out at a separate warehouse in Fort de France which, impressively, can handle up to 2 million litres of ageing rum at any given time.

EL DORADO Guyana

SUPERIOR WHITE
(37.5, 40 and 43 per cent abv)
Pedigree rum blended solely
from three to six month old,
cask-matured rums. Delicate,
sweet aroma with a subtle,
extra-light flavour. The "White
Gold" of Guyana.

GOLDEN **(37.5 and 40 per cent abv)**
Oak-aged for six months. Light and distinctively
dry with an oaky, fruity nose, mellow taste and
smooth finish.

DARK
(37.5 and 40 per cent abv)
Mellow, characterful, two-year-old blend. Balance
between gentleness and strength with a rounded,
sweet caramel nose and a warm, rich, full-bodied
taste.

FIVE-YEAR-OLD **(40 and 43 per cent abv)**
Premium blend with a distinctive, delicate taste.
Aged in 45-gallon oak casks.

12-YEAR-OLD (40 per cent abv)
Smooth premium rum with full, fragrant aroma and opulent taste.

SPECIAL RESERVE 15-YEAR-OLD (43 per cent abv)
Top of the range, complex, brandy-like, dark blend of great distinction. Made from selected rums matured in 45-gallon oak casks. Walnut and date flavours abound, yet it is soft, silky and gentle. Blended, bottled and packaged exclusively at Demerara Distillers in Guyana. The custom-designed bottle was inspired by the shape of the old hand-blown flasks used over three centuries ago by the early sugar planters.

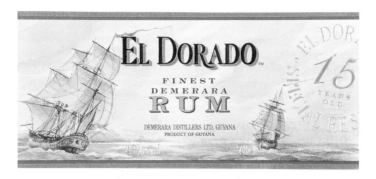

See also Demerara Distillers

ENGLISH HARBOUR Antigua

See Antigua Distillery

E.S.A. FIELDS Barbados
(43 per cent abv)

See Stade's

ESPÈRANCE-MON REPOS DISTILLERY Guadeloupe

Established 1895 at Domaine du Marquisat de Ste. Marie. Under the export label of Longueteau, makes unaged, 50 per cent abv white and seven-year-old vieux from the fresh juice of year-old cane, distilled in a copper and stainless steel, single-column still.

EXPEDITION SUPERIOR LIGHT
(37.5 per cent abv)

See Hall & Bramley

FERNANDES DISTILLERS Trinidad

Founded in the 1920s by Jo Fernandes but now a subsidiary of Angostura. At one stage, he couldn't make enough rum for his blends, so he bought Trinidad rum in England and shipped it back.

CRYSTAL WHITE (43 per cent abv)
Very light-bodied, very smooth and very clear.

FORRES PARK PUNCHEON (75 per cent abv)
Clear, light rum named after the old sugar estate and distillery where the business started in the 1920s.

VAT 19 WHITE
(37.5, 40 and 43 per cent abv)
Blend of three- and four-year-old rums. Medium-dry style with a well-balanced, sumptuous taste. Also bottled under licence in Canada.

WHITE STAR (40 and 43 per cent abv)
Smooth, light-bodied amber rum. Blend of mature light and heavy rums coloured with caramel to enhance the gentle hues taken from the wood.

VAT 19 GOLD
(37.5, 40 and 43 per cent abv)
"The carnival spirit of Trinidad" captured in a bottle and the flagship label of Fernandes. Blend of three- and four-year-old light and heavy types giving a weighty, medium-dry rum with a complex, tarry nose and smooth, rich, toast-and-liquorice flavours. Also bottled under licence in Canada and Scotland.

BL – Black Label (43 per cent abv)
Blend of golden and dark rums. A higher proportion of the former gives a smooth, light body.

Ferdi's Premium (43 per cent abv)
Top blend of very mature, light and heavy type rums. Rich, dark colour but medium-bodied with a notably mellow texture.
See also Angostura, Seagram

FLOR DE CAÑA Nicaragua

Most significant brand of Compañia Licorera de Nicaragua, the only distillery of note in Nicaragua. A joint production venture was established with the Compañia Liquorera Los Angeles in Honduras in 1971.

Exported to 19 countries, Flor de Caña comes in a range of 40 per cent abv, molasses-based, five-column-distilled rums aged in 185-litre white oak barrels, characterised by very floral aromas, mildness and lightness of weight and a long, buttery, sweet finish.

Four basic styles: Extra Lite four-year-old; Extra Seco Reserva Especial four-year-old; Elite Oro four-year-old; and Black Label five-year-old. Grand Reserve seven-year-old is the upmarket label, nicely balanced with a vanilla and citrus nose and silky flavours. Centenario 12-year-old is the premium style.

GOSLING'S BLACK SEAL

(40 and 75.5 per cent abv)

In 1806, English wine and spirit merchant James Gosling set out to sea with ten thousand pounds' worth of merchandise bound for Virginia. Becalmed after 91 desperate days, the ship put in at the nearest port, St George's, Bermuda. Rather than pressing on to America, Gosling opened a shop. His brother Ambrose took over the enterprise and, in 1857, the firm was renamed Gosling Brothers. Three years later, they imported the island's first barrels of Caribbean rum and, after much experimentation with the blending, Black Seal, first known as "Old Rum", was born.

At first, it was sold only on draught. It was then put into champagne bottles and the corks were

made fast with black sealing wax – hence the name. Having said that, black by name, black by nature – this rum has a deep, coffee-coloured, almost black appearance.

Today, this premium style is still carefully blended to the family's original, secret recipe from imported three-year-old rums. A medley of aromas – plum, quinine, juniper, cedar, coffee, cola and resin – followed by intensely spicy and rich flavours and a long, smooth, sweet finish of sugar cane and tropical fruits. A truly complex, assertive, highly flavoured and full-bodied rum.

Over the years, Black Seal has become has become synonymous with Bermuda. It's an essential ingredient in Bermuda fish chowder, adds the island flavour to Bermuda Rum Swizzle and is the tempest in Bermuda's favourite cocktail, the Dark 'n' Stormy (Black Seal and ginger beer). The name is said to have been invented by an old sailor who observed that the drink was the "colour of a cloud only a fool or a dead man would sail under". (This was probably followed by, "Barman, I'll have another"!)

Gosling's also blend and market Gosling's Barbados Rum at 40 and 75.5 per cent abv.

HALL & BRAMLEY UK

Part of Halewood International (UK) Ltd and an important blender and bottler of rum to the UK market. Imports rum from Barbados, Guyana, Réunion and other Caribbean islands in container or cask. Besides its own brands, H&B blends and bottles rums under contract for companies in the UK and elsewhere.

One of their brands, Expedition Superior Light (37.5 per cent abv), is the second most popular white rum brand in the UK's take-home trade. Made from rums from Guyana and Barbados, it is delicately flavoured, light and zesty.

HAVANA CLUB Cuba

Born in 1878 and produced by the Pernod-Ricard group in joint venture with

Cubaron since 1993, though Havana Club manages production. The only major brand in Cuba, it's also exported to Canada, France, Germany, Ireland, Italy, Mexico, Spain (the biggest market after Cuba), the UK and throughout Latin America.

All styles are made in a continuous still, claimed to be the slowest in world. By law, they are then aged for at least 18 months in 180-litre vats made of American white oak.

SILVER DRY (37.5 per cent abv)

The most widely consumed of the family. White blend where the effects

of the required minimum ageing period shine through. Mild, delicate, dry yet warm taste with strokes of citrus and coconut and a fresh cane aftertaste.

THREE-YEAR-OLD
(40 per cent abv)
Light-amber colour with a subtle, banana, apple brandy-styled nose and a sweet toffee and spice taste that finishes dry. Chewy but delightfully light.

FIVE-YEAR-OLD (40 per cent abv)
Subtle aroma but rich, strong flavour.

Above

La Bodeguita del Medio in Havana, one of Cuba's most famous bars – immortalised by the words of Hemingway: "My mojito in da Bodeguita/ My daiquiri in El Floridita."

AÑEJO RESERVA (40 per cent abv)

Dark gold seven-year-old combining the characteristic nose of an aged rum with the lightness associated with a white. Attractively spicy and sweet in aroma and powerfully bodied. It has a nutty, butterscotch-flavoured start and a smooth, vanilla-tinged finish.

EXQUISITO (40 per cent abv)

Duty-free brand launched in 1998. Currently exclusive to World Brands, the duty-free arm of Pernod-Ricard, although it may be rolled out into domestic markets later. This is an aged rum although there's no age statement on the label.

J. BALLY Martinique

Made from fermented juice of sugar cane grown at the 70-year-old Lajus plantation. Fermentation is carried out under contract by Distillerie Simon, where J. Bally also house their copper, single-column still. The *vieux rhums* must be aged for at least three years before release, and this must be carried out in 180-litre Limousin or American oak casks. Some rum is then transferred into 600-litre casks for slower maturation. This is called "*mise en vieillissement*" and the vintage indicates the year of transfer rather than the year of distillation. Colour comes solely from the maturation process. Likened in taste and texture to good armagnac, it is expensive, but still good value by comparison. The brand is owned by Rémy & Associates.

Grappe Blanche
(50 per cent abv)
Popular unaged white. Also bottle *rhums agricoles blancs* at 45, 55 and 62 per cent abv plus a Coeur du Chauffe at 55 per cent abv.

Rhum Paille
(50 per cent abv)
A straw-coloured, two year old.

Rhum Vieux
(45 per cent abv)
Aged for six years. Bottled in 1997.

J. Bally 1986
(45 per cent abv)
Deep gold colour. Deceptively sweet on the nose, rich and honeyed. Spicy, complex, oaky flavours.

J. Bally 1970 (45 per cent abv)
Gold amber colour. Orange peel nose with

hints of toffee. Rich, lingering flavours with touches of spice and fruit.

See Distillerie Simon

J. WRAY & NEPHEW
Jamaica

Oldest and largest producer in Jamaica, founded 1825, making a variety of blends under Appleton, Coruba and Wray & Nephew labels. These molasses and cane juice-based rums are blended from the distillate of two- or three-column stills or copper pot stills. Ageing is carried out in American oak. W&N rums are exported to over 60 different countries. Bottlers abroad maintain the specifications and standards laid down by the distillery. Mexico is the company's premier export market. Subsidiaries in the UK and New Zealand.

See also Appleton, C.J. Wray; Coruba, Wray & Nephew Overproof

LA MAUNY Martinique

The *rhums agricoles* of this 200-year-old property are a favourite in Martinique, characterised by their aroma of freshly cut sugar cane and very fruity taste. Forty per cent of the sugar cane requirement comes from La Mauny estate, the

Opposite
With its
mountainous
rain forest and
narrow valleys
lined with fertile
volcanic soils,
Martinique has
a reputation for
rich, pungent
rums.

balance being supplied by local, independent producers. The domestic market represents around 50 per cent of sales. The rest is exported mainly to France, but also to Africa, Belgium, Canada, Germany, Japan, Netherlands, Sweden and Tahiti.

Formerly a sugar refinery, the distillery was built by Count Joseph Ferdinand Poulain who moved to Martinique from France in 1749. After several changes of ownership, it is now controlled by Bellonie-Bourdillon et Successeurs. Theirs is a huge and diverse operation. In addition to being the largest distiller of rhum agricole in the Caribbean (to put this into perspective, they distil in excess of 35,000 litres of rum a day – more than some distillers can make in a year), the company owns rice paddies in Guyana and also acts as the agent for l'Oréal products in the French islands.

RHUM BLANC DES PLANTATIONS
(40 to 62 per cent abv)
Three months ageing in 50,000-litre oak vats. Highly perfumed and very delicate in taste.

RHUM DORÉ (43 per cent abv)
Blend of golden rums aged for a minimum of 12 years with a mellow, woody flavour.

RHUMS VIEUX (45 per cent abv)
Three-, five- and seven-year-old blends matured in 250-litre, ex-cognac or bourbon, recharred oak casks.

RHUM VIEUX VSOP (43 per cent abv)
Four-year-old.

RHUM VIEUX XO (43 per cent abv)
Six-year-old.

RHUM VIEUX HORS D'AGE (43 per cent abv)
Ten-year-old.

RHUMS VIEUX 1979 AND 1987 (43 per cent abv)
Limited release, numbered bottles.

LAMB'S

In 1849, Alfred Lamb opened a wine and spirit
business in London. He soon began to import
casks of rum for ageing in his cool and humid
cellars beneath the River Thames in London
which gave his rums great appeal. Now bottled at
various sites around the world by, or for, Allied
Domecq. In Canada, for instance, the trademark
is owned by Corby Distillers who have exclusive
rights to produce, market and sell it within
Canada. Fifty per cent of Corby, however, is
owned by Hiram Walker who, in turn, is wholly
owned by Allied. In Kenya, International
Distillers manufactures Lamb's Navy and Lamb's
White under licence.

LAMB'S WHITE (40 per cent abv)
The third best-selling white rum in Canada
where it is made and sold.

LAMB'S PALM BREEZE (40 per cent abv)
Best-selling amber rum in Canada. Rich in
weight, but has a fruity, light caramel edge and
chocolate smokiness.

LAMB'S NAVY (40 per cent abv)
Very traditional, premium quality dark rum brand of international renown. A smooth and mellow blend of molasses-based, pot and column-distilled rums from Barbados, Guyana, Jamaica and Trinidad; it has an irresistible aroma and flavour of fruit, oak and burnt toffee with a very long, sweet finish.

LAMB'S RESERVE
(40 per cent abv)
Copper pot-still rum with a little column-still rum added, aged for a minimum of eight years. Remarkably similar to cognac – delicate with a honeyed, oaky complexity.

LAMB'S OVERPROOF
(75.4 per cent abv)
Two styles, Navy and White, produced in Canada, mainly for duty-free sales.

LANG'S FINEST OLD BANANA
Jamaica (40 per cent abv)
Top-notch golden rum imported to and bottled in the UK by Lang Brothers Ltd for home sales

and re-export. A pot-still distillation of sugar and molasses giving full aroma and firm character.

La Tondeña
Philippines

Division of San Miguel Corporation, the Philippines' leading food and beverage conglomerate and undisputed market leader of distilled liquors.

Makes molasses-based, oak-aged rums: vibrant, light yet full-bodied Añejo 65 (32.5 per cent abv); light-bodied Añejo Oro (40 per cent abv); medium-bodied, aromatic and dry Añejo Five Star (40 per cent abv); mellow Añejo Five Year Old Black (40 per cent abv); very light Manila Silver (one year in wood; 40 per cent abv); Manila Gold (three years of ageing; 40 per cent abv); full-flavoured, medium-bodied Manila Dark (four-year-old; 40 per cent abv); Manila Añejo (matured for five years; 40 per cent abv). Popular locally and the Manila labels are also found overseas, particularly in the USA and Canada.

LEMON HART (40 per cent abv)
One of the most dashing characters in rum history was Mr Lemon Hart whose grandfather started trading Demeraran rum in 1720 from Cornwall, England. His grandson inherited the business which by then had been appointed victualler to the Royal Navy. In 1804 Lemon Hart moved the business to the West India Docks in London.

A traditional, heavy-bodied blend of Guyanan and Jamaican rums, still aged and bottled in the UK, this is one of the most pungent dark rums on offer. Deep in colour, it sports an aggressive flavour with smoky notes. It is the leading imported rum in Canada.

LONGUETEAU Guadeloupe

See Espèrance-Mon Repos

MAINSTAY South Africa
(43 per cent abv)
First marketed in the early 1950s to take advantage of the very healthy take-home market in cane spirit, a result of the shortage of imported spirits during the Second World War. Using the name "Mainstay" was a bold risk because it was traditionally used as a generic term – like Umhali Water or Gavine – for any old cane spirit, good or bad. Well, it obviously worked because it's now South Africa's leading spirit brand. Also sold

elsewhere in Africa and made under licence in Mauritius by Grays & Co.

MALIBU COCONUT   Barbados
(24 per cent abv)
Launched into a very buoyant speciality drinks market in 1980, this has become the world's fifth fastest-growing brand and is placed in the top 70 drinks' brands. The statistics are phenomenal: over 1.7 million cases are sold around the world each year and, by the end of 1996, over 130

million bottles had been sold. It's a fun drink designed to capture the carefree spontaneity of the Caribbean lifestyle. A deliciously clear blend of coconut, sugar and white rum from the West Indies Rum Distillery. You can drink it neat with ice, or long with a host of suitable mixers (in Prague they even drink it with milk). It's also invaluable for those of us who are fond of the odd Piña Colada. Forty per cent of the brand's sales are in the UK and France.

There's also Malibu Lime (24 per cent abv), launched in France in 1995, with lime in place of coconut giving a slightly more challenging flavour; and Malibu Spice (5.5 per cent abv) – "ready-mixed" style launched in the UK in 1997 to replace Malibu Cocktails.

See also West Indies Rum Distillery

MATUSALEM Puerto Rico

Founded in 1872 by Benjamin and Eduardo Camp in Santiago de Cuba producing what became known as the cognac of rums. "*Esto es mas viejo que Matusalem*" ("it's older than Methuselah"), referring to the use of very old rums in their blends. Some of these are aged using a special "solera" system. When rum from the oldest cask is drawn off for blending and bottling, the cask is topped up with a slightly younger rum. Magically, the younger rum acquires the characteristics of the older rum remaining in the barrel. In turn, the cask from which the younger rum was taken is topped up with an even younger rum. And so on. It's a very clever method of promoting consistency of flavour and style in the finished blend.

The family was exiled in 1960 and now distils molasses-based rums in Puerto Rico. These are aged, blended and bottled either in the Bahamas and Miami for the big North American market, or at Distillerie Smeets in the Netherlands for the European market.

There are five styles, all characterised by their delicate qualities:

CARTA PLATA (40 per cent abv)
Very light and dry.

CARTA ORO (40 per cent abv)
Five-year-old solera blend.

CLASSIC BLACK (40 per cent abv)
Dark, full-bodied and exceptionally smooth, seven-year-old solera blend.

GRAN RESERVA (40 per cent abv)
Super-premium, 15-year-old blend launched 1997.

RED FLAME (75.5 per cent abv)
Hot by name and hot by nature. The fiery

strength of this otherwise unremarkable rum adds a kick to any exotic drink.

MONTEBELLO Guadeloupe

Made at the Carrère distillery, founded in 1930 and owned by the Marsolle family, who have a hand in a number of distilleries in Guadeloupe. They use cane from their own fields, buying in the balance required, and produce *rhums agricoles* using a copper, two-column still. Sold locally and distributed in France (by Bardinet) and the USA.

UNAGED RHUM BLANC (50 and 55 per cent abv)
Particularly perfumed style, scented with sweet and subtle aromas of freshly cut sugar cane.

RHUM VIEUX (42 per cent abv)
Available as a four-, six- or ten-year-old, aged in 190-litre oak casks. Delicate, golden rums of great character boasting wonderful aromas of vanilla and wood and strong, warm, tropical spice flavours with good length.

See also Bardinet

MOUNT GAY Barbados

Dating from 1663, one of the oldest estates in the Caribbean and certainly the oldest in Barbados. Owned then by Dr William Gay, thought to be a cousin of John Gay who wrote *The Beggar's Opera*.

Produces various styles characterised by unique, smoky, deep, elegant and relatively dry flavours. Molasses is fermented with a special yeast and then distilled either twice in a copper pot still or once in a two-column continuous still. Maturation is carried out in slightly charred, 200-litre, hand-crafted, ex-Bourbon casks and only pure, underground, coral-filtered spring water is used throughout.

Mount Gay rums were introduced to the international market in 1926 by Aubrey Ward, said to be the father of around a hundred children! Today, global sales are handled by Rémy & Associates who own 60 per cent of the company.

Mount Gay Premium White
(40 and 43 per cent abv)
Light-bodied style blended from filtered two-year-old rums.

Mount Gay Refined Eclipse
(37.5, 40, 43 and 77 per cent abv)
Flagship, medium-bodied blend of two-year-old pot and continuous still rums. Inviting, vibrant, golden-

amber colour. Subtle, lightly smoky aromas of nuts, biscuits, burnt sugar, apricots and vanilla. Complex, well-balanced, soft fruit and oak flavours with a long-lasting, slightly sweet aftertaste.

MOUNT GAY SUGAR CANE (43 per cent abv)
Strong reflection of sugar cane in this deep, amber-coloured blend of rums up to seven years old. Sweet oak and spice-and-fruit nose with a warm, smooth, rich and woody flavour. Not available in the UK.

MOUNT GAY EXTRA OLD (40 and 43 per cent abv)
Premium, amber-brown fusion of finest single and double-distilled rums selected from Mount Gay's five- to 12-year-old aged reserves. Light, burnt-wood nose, a rich, oaky taste balanced by sweet banana, vanilla, apricot and caramel flavours. A delicate rum from nose to finish, it's rather whisky-like in character.

MYERS'S Jamaica
The bronze-coloured, molasses-based, pot-still Myers's Planter's Punch (40 per cent abv) is the number one premium imported dark rum in America. Famous for its rich, cedary, almost treacly character, it boasts an overpowering, smoky tobacco nose with aromas of citrus, black pepper, cayenne and anise, an overture to strong

notes of clove and chocolate and a lean, semi-sweet finish. Made from a blend of up to nine select rums matured for up to four years in white oak.

In response to the worldwide penchant for lightness, Myers's Platinum White (40 per cent abv) is currently being test-marketed in selected US states. Distilled in Puerto Rico, it's more robust than most other Puerto Rican rums.

See also Seagram

NATIONAL RUMS OF JAMAICA

Operate a distillery as part of the National Sugar Company Ltd. Column-distilled rums are sold in bulk to other blenders and bottlers on the island and overseas.

NEGRITA Martinique

See Dillon

OCUMARE Venezuela

Launched in 1995 by United Distillers in Venezuela, Canada, Mexico, Peru, the UK and the USA. Unaged Blanco Especial (40 per cent abv) and three-year-old, golden, sipping style

Añejo Especial (40 per cent abv) are both infused with guarana, a seed found in the Amazon basin and whose properties are not dissimilar to those of ginseng. Very contemporary packaging promotes a stylish, exotic, adventurous image.

OLD BRIGAND
Barbados

Filtered White and coloured Black blends of 40 per cent abv rums less than five years old available under the old Arthur Alleyne label, but blended by R.L. Seale & Co. Ltd. Bottled at 43 per cent abv for the export market (particularly popular in Canada). Another primary export brand, Black Label Superior (37, 40 and 43 per cent abv), is a blend of rums aged for up to 13 years.

See also R.L. Seale

OLD NICK
Martinique

See Dillon

OLD OAK Trinidad
(43 per cent abv)
Leading brand in Trinidad and Tobago but also exported. Two styles: White and Gold, both unaged and delicate in style.

See also Angostura

ORO AÑEJO RESERVA
Colombia
(38 per cent abv)
Twelve-year-old blend produced by Licores de los Andes.

O.V.D. Guyana
(40 per cent abv)
Old Vatted Demerara, as its name implies, is blended from the finest Demeraran rums matured for up to seven years. It was first imported in 1838 by the George Morton Company, now owned by Seagram, and is now the UK's third most popular dark rum after Captain Morgan and Lamb's Navy. Very dark in colour, but light and smooth on the tongue with a distinctive fruity flavour. Slightly sweeter than most dark rums. Try it with peppermint, orange or blackcurrant.

PALO VIEJO (Puerto Rico)

See Serrallés

PAMPERO Venezuela

Industrias Pampero, founded in 1930s by Alejandro Gernandez, is the second-largest rum producer in the world. Very little was exported, however, until acquisition of the company by United Distillers in 1991. Now, over 20 countries import Pampero rums.

PAMPERO AÑEJO ESPECIAL (40 per cent abv)

In 1942, Industrias Pampero pioneered the ageing of rum in small 500-litre oak barrels. Subsequently, two-, three- and four-year-old rums were introduced, the first legally aged rums in Venezuela. The range was wound down in the 1970s and all efforts went into this label.

PAMPERO ANIVERSARIO CONNOISSEUR'S (40 per cent abv)

Premium rum, aged six years plus, made to celebrate Industrias Pampero's 25th anniversary. Amber-orange in colour, has a cognac-like nose of oak and vanilla with allspice and caramel flavours tempered by a woody bite and an intense, sweet, cherryish finish. Marketed in numbered bottles that come in a soft leather pouch, this is a truly fine sipping rum of great depth and complexity.

PÈRE LABAT
Marie Galante

Made at Distillerie Poisson that started life as a sugar mill in 1860. They still have 120 hectares of sugar cane from which *rhums agricoles* are made in a copper, single-column still. Marketed in Marie Galante, Canada, France, Guadeloupe and Sint Maarten.

LA GUILDIVE
(59 per cent abv)
Young white aged in 10,000-litre oak casks for one month.

RHUM DORÉ
(50 per cent abv).
Blend of white and three-year-old *rhums agricoles.*

RHUM PAILLE
(50 per cent abv)
Two-year-old bottled for Europe and Canada only.

RHUM VIEUX
(45 per cent abv)
Aged in 200-litre, ex-Bourbon casks and not distributed before six years old.

PIRASSUNUNGA 51 Brazil
(40 per cent abv)

Brazil's leading cachaça and the only one of over 600 formal brands to be exported in any serious volume; indeed, depending on which statistics you believe, it may even beat Bacardi as the biggest spirit brand in the world. Either way, it's right up there in the superleague and is now found in more than 27 countries, though distiller Industrias Muller de Bebidas is currently promoting an aggressive campaign with the long-term goal of establishing sales in a further 33 countries. Having said that, exports currently represent less than 1 per cent of the brand's total sales.

PUSSER'S PREMIUM NAVY
(54.5 per cent abv)

Ten years after the abolition of the Royal Navy rum ration in 1970, ex-US Marine and enterprising businessman Charles Tobias hit upon the idea of recreating and commercially marketing the standard issue rum that was used for the daily tot. The Admiralty approved and Pusser's Navy Rum was launched.

Expertly blended from six different aged pot-still rums originating in Trinidad, Guyana and Tortola (British Virgin Islands), this bottled liquid history offers the ultimate in old-fashioned, honey-rich, dark rums – a very individual and exotic bouquet backed by distinctive, complex and massive flavours. Some say that its taste is unsurpassed.

It is now owned by Jim Beam Brands who have maintained the tradition of making a substantial royalty donation to the Royal Navy Sailors' Fund (the "Tot Fund") for every bottle sold worldwide in appreciation of the Admiralty Board's permission to blend Pusser's Rum to their original formula.

RIVER ANTOINE ROYALE GRENADIAN Grenada

(83 per cent abv)

Founded in 1785, this distillery uses traditional machinery including a huge waterwheel that powers the crushing mills. Fresh cane juice is fermented with natural yeasts for eight days (a long time by normal standards) and then pot-distilled. The high demand for this rum precludes any ageing so it's white in colour and, no doubt because this is the way the locals like to drink it, they don't bother to water it down. Incidentally, this was the very first high-strength-whopping-impact rum I ever tasted and it was certainly hard work standing up afterwards!

R.L. SEALE & CO. Barbados

Wholly Bajan-owned, 17th-century Hopefield estate and the third-largest blender and bottler in Barbados. Raw rum is currently bought from the West Indies Rum Distillery, but a distillery of their own was commissioned in 1996. Acquired Alleyne Arthur & Hunte in 1993.

See also Doorly's, Old Brigand, Special Barbados, Stade's, West Indies Rum Distillery

RON CARIOCA US Virgin Islands

Easy-drinking, dry Blanco, light Oro and smooth Dark, made by the Carioca Rum Company in St Croix, all at 40 per cent abv. Some exported in bulk for bottling elsewhere (to Canada, for example).

RON GRANADO Puerto Rico

See Serrallés

RON LLAVE BLANCO SUPREMO Puerto Rico

See Serrallés

RONRICO Puerto Rico

See Serrallés

ROYAL OAK SELECT Trinidad
(43 per cent abv)
Deluxe blend of oak-aged golden rums. Shows a gentle mellowness and attractive balance. Each bottle is registered by the master blender.

See also Angostura

SAINT-JAMES Martinique
Oldest distillery on the island, built in 1765 by Father Lefébure of the Charity Brothers as part of the Saint-James Sugar Factory, but forced to

relocate to the other side of the island following the 1902 eruption of Mount Pelée. Today, it has the second-largest distilling capacity in Martinique and is now owned by Rémy & Associates.

Produces *rhums agricoles* of great finesse, some 60 per cent of which are exported to France and other parts of Europe, Africa, Asia, Australasia, North and South America. Rhum Millésime is also made, although I haven't tracked down any beyond 1976. Saint-James also bulk exports molasses-based rums for French own-labels.

RHUM IMPERIAL BLANC
(40, 50 and 55 per cent abv)
Unaged rum stored in stainless steel for six months before bottling.

COEUR DU CHAUFFE (60 and 62 per cent abv)
Unaged white, pot-still rum. Produced in tiny quantities.

RHUM PAILLE (45 per cent abv)
Eighteen months' maturation in 35,000-litre Limousin oak casks.

RHUM AMBRÉ (45, 50 and 55 per cent abv)
Two-year-old combining the richness of an old rum and the freshness of a white.

RHUM VIEUX (40, 42 and 45 per cent abv)
Aged for three years in 200-litre Limousin oak barrels.

RHUM VIEUX HORS D'AGE
(43 and 45 per cent abv)
Premium blend of aged rums of at least three years in age. Heady, rich aroma and, as Saint-James themselves boast, "a taster's treasure".

SANGSTER'S Jamaica

Located high up in the Blue Mountains, Sangster's was created in 1974 by Scottish immigrant Dr Ian Sangster. They age and blend their own fine rums plus a range of exotic, rum-based liqueurs using home-produced natural essences and extracts.

CONQUERING LION **(64 per cent abv)**
Smooth white rum. Found in the UK.

GOLD DELUXE **(40 to 57 per cent abv)**
Contains a high percentage of richly flavoured pot-still rums carefully blended with lighter rums to yield a mellow, smooth drink with a distinctive bouquet and taste.

SANTA TERESA Venezuela

Fifth-largest world seller by volume though most is sold on the domestic market.

SEAGRAM

This Canadian giant first became interested in rum in 1943, forming the Captain Morgan Rum Company in Jamaica for the international

marketing of the Captain Morgan brand. They purchased the Long Pond estate and distillery ten years later as a source of raw material to satisfy growing demand.

In 1955, they bought Myers's, Jamaica's largest-selling brand and, in 1959, acquired Wood & Company (Wood's 100 Old Navy and White Sail). In addition, Seagram owns the George Morton Company, Scotland's leading rum specialist (O.V.D.) and Serrallés (Puerto Rico). Makes various brands for the Canadian market and Cacique in Venezuela.

Included in Seagram's remit are the world agency rights to both the Monymusk distillery in Jamaica (in conjunction with the Jamaican government) and Demerara Distillers' Diamond Distillery in Guyana. Seagram also bottles Vat 19 in Canada and Scotland under licence for Fernandes Distillers. Seagram UK is the UK's leading producer of dark rums.

See also Cacique, Captain Morgan, Fernandes, Myers's, O.V.D., Serrallés, Wood's

SEE THROUGH Barbados
(43 per cent abv)

See Stade's

Opposite
Myers's, Jamaica's favourite rum, was bought by the Canadian giant, Seagram, in 1955.

SERRALLÉS Puerto Rico

One of Puerto Rico's two surviving operating distilleries, founded by Sebastian Serrallés in the late 19th century and run by the family for many generations, but now owned by Seagram. Along with manufacture of gin, vodka and other neutral spirits for use in liqueurs, Serrallés produces rums for both local and US brands.

DON Q

Aged blends sold at home and in Canada, Mexico, Spain and the USA under four labels: Cristal White (largest-selling rum in Puerto Rico, slightly fuller than Bacardi; 40 per cent abv); 151 Overproof (75.5 per cent abv); Gold (40 per cent abv); and Gran Añejo (40 per cent abv). This last is a recent addition to the portfolio – a premium blend of three- to 12-year-old rums, including some that are aged in old sherry casks by way of a solera system.

PALO VIEJO (40 per cent abv)

Distilled for the US market.

RON GRANADO (40 per cent abv)

White rum for the USA.

RON LLAVE BLANCO SUPREMO (40 per cent abv)

Bottled in the USA. Distinct nose of sugar cane and slightly warm on the tongue.

RONRICO (40 per cent abv)
One-hundred-and-thirty-year-old brand noted for its smooth yet bold flavours. Three labels: Silver (premium white dry; 40 per cent abv); Gold (premium; smooth; dry; number four selling brand in the USA; 40 per cent abv); Purple (mainly used for cooking; 75.5 per cent abv). Bottled by Jim Beam Brands in the USA.

See also Captain Morgan, Seagram

SIKKIM India

Some people are amazing. Jimmy Contractor (*sic*) built five distilleries only to lose everything in the 1946 Prohibition. He then set up a plywood factory and mill that were destroyed in an earthquake. Having rebuilt once more, his efforts were washed away in a flood two years later. Undeterred, he helped to establish a distillery in Sikkim in the eastern Himalayas in 1955 and went on to build two more in Nepal and Bhutan.

The rums are mainly column-distilled from fermented cane juice known as "jaggery". All possess a robust character. Well liked within India, exports are also made to Australasia, Germany, Holland, the Middle East, Papua New Guinea, the UK and the USA.

TEESTA XXX
(42.8 per cent abv)
Named after the river flowing through the Himalayas. Unusual in that it's the redistillate of well-matured dark rum. This removes colour and excesses of flavour leaving a white rum of some weight.

XXX PRIZE (42.8 per cent abv) Golden rum of nine months ageing. Full-flavoured but lighter in style to Black Cat.

BLACK CAT (42.8 per cent abv) Golden rum with full body and richness from three to five years in wood. Introduced in 1963 to honour the name of one of the divisions of the Indian Army.

STRIKING LION (42.8 per cent abv) Full-bodied, five-year-old golden blend. Mostly column still with some pot still.

SPECIAL BARBADOS
Barbados
(40 per cent abv)
Blend of exquisitely balanced, medium-bodied rums up to five years in age, bottled under the old Arthur Alleyne label. Primarily exported to Europe.

See also R.L. Seale

SQUADRON (45 per cent abv)

Dark rum, rich in taste and flavour, blended by Gilbey Distillers & Vintners, South Africa from local rectified spirit and imported, one-year-old Jamaican rum. Also Squadron White and Squadron Leader. Distributed in South Africa, Nigeria and Uganda.

STADE'S Barbados
(43 per cent abv)

Aged white, also known as E.S.A. Field or See Through, the bestselling white rum in Barbados. Occasionally spotted abroad.

See also R.L. Seale

TANDUAY Philippines

Huge brand worldwide from one of the biggest distilleries of the islands. With a history spanning 140 years, it boasts a tradition of quality and excellence. Tanduay has three separate plants plus a storage facility for no fewer than 35,000 barrels. Export markets include Australia, Hong Kong, Japan, Malaysia, Russia, Singapore, Thailand and the USA. Available in all styles – the exact names on the labels vary according to where you buy it – made from a ruthless selection of natural ingredients. Ageing takes place in charred, 200-litre, white oak barrels. And to quote Tanduay themselves, their rum certainly "pours on the good times".

TODHUNTER INTERNATIONAL
USA

Nationally recognised distiller, bottler, wine producer and manufacturer of fine food with headquarters in Florida. Florida Distillers Company is the division that handles rum, built in the Second World War to make industrial alcohol from fruit for the war effort. Bottle Puerto Rican and Virgin Island rums under contract for the US market. Another branch, Todhunter Imports, imports and markets rums from the Virgin Islands Rum Distillery Company that it owns.

See Cruzan

TRINIDAD DISTILLERS **Trinidad**

A subsidiary of Angostura Holdings in which Bacardi has a 40 per cent stake. Buys molasses from the Caroni Sugar Factory.

See also Angostura

TROIS-RIVIÈRES **Martinique**

See Duquesne-Trois-Rivières

VAT 19 **Trinidad**

See Fernandes

Above

Port of Spain, Trinidad c.1860, a major centre for the rum industry then and now.

VIEJO DE CALDAS Colombia

Premium, three-year-old, cane juice-based, after-dinner golden rum of unusual complexity. Bouquet of fried bananas and spring flowers with liquorice and anise flavours and a burnt sugar finish. Exported to the USA.

VIRGIN ISLANDS RUM DISTILLERY US Virgin Islands

See Cruzan, Todhunter

WEST INDIES RUM DISTILLERY Barbados

Doesn't bottle rum under its own name, but is hugely important as it distils just about all Bajan rum with the exception of Mount Gay. Molasses is fermented for five days followed by distillation in a four-column still, though a little is pot-distilled. The rum is either bulk-shipped directly to the customer at this point or put into uncharred, ex-Bourbon casks for ageing on their behalf.

See also Cockspur, Malibu, R.L. Seale

WESTERHALL ESTATE Grenada

Takes pride in traditional methods of production. Distributed in Canada, Switzerland (for Europe), the USA and the US Virgin Islands plus mail order around the world.

Superb Light (43 per cent abv)
Three-year-old blend with a distinctive mellow flavour.

Rum Sipper Strong (70 per cent abv)
Traditional, hearty, full-flavoured, overproof pot-still white rum distilled from cane juice. Enjoyed "straight up" by the locals.

Plantation (43 per cent abv)
Smooth sipping rum from pot-distilled cane juice blended with golden rum. Westerhall's premium blend.

WHITE STAR Trinidad

See Fernandes

WOOD'S 100 OLD NAVY
Guyana (57 per cent abv)

Extra-strength, finest, dark pot-still Demerara rums blended in the UK and Canada by Seagram. Dimensions of coffee, spice and toffee in a rich, full-bodied style. Historically Wood's was enjoyed by the Royal Navy "dockside".

Also Wood's White Sail (40 per cent abv), blended in Canada by Seagram for the local market.

See also Seagram

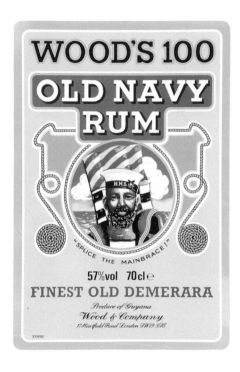

WRAY & NEPHEW WHITE OVERPROOF Jamaica

(62.8 per cent abv)

World's bestselling overproof rum blended from both light and full-flavoured styles. Accounts for over 90 per cent of the rum consumed in Jamaica ... it scares off the duppies (see Chapter 2)! As master blender Owen Tulloch puts it, "Heat up some milk, add a touch of nutmeg, throw in some OP and you won't need a coat to go out in the snow!". Pungent aromas of fruit and burnt sugar with smooth, complex flavours, a touch of aniseed and overtones of molasses.

See also J. Wray & Nephew

YPIÓCA Brazil

Popular brand of cane spirit, progeny of the sugar plantation and refinery bought by the Telles family in Fortaleza in 1846. Four styles made in a modified variation of a Portuguese pot still: two-year-old white Empalhada Plata; two-year-old golden Empalhada Ouro; four-year-old golden Conta-Gotas; six-year-old golden 150. Exported to Europe, Japan and the USA.

CHAPTER SIX

CLASSIC RUM COCKTAILS

DAIQUIRI

This cocktail was officially christened by a group of American engineers working in the Daiquiri tin mines near Santiago de Cuba at the turn of the century. They regularly imbibed this potion for medicinal purposes – or so they alleged!

Serves 1
5cl (1 ^{2}/3 fl oz) white rum
3cl (1 fl oz) fresh lime juice
grenadine to taste

Shake all ingredients together and serve very cold with a twist of lime.

RUM PUNCH

1 Sour; 2 Sweet; 3 Strong; 4 Weak – there are plenty of adaptations for this famous formula, but here's a colourful one.

Serves 1
1cl (^{1}/3 fl oz) fresh lime juice
2cl (^{2}/3 fl oz) grenadine

Opposite
Rum is one of the best spirit bases for a whole range of cocktails. White rum is traditionally used but golden rum is excellent too.

3cl (1 fl oz) golden rum
2cl (²/3 fl oz) pineapple juice
2cl (²/3 fl oz) orange juice
Angostura bitters to taste

Stir all the ingredients together with lots of crushed ice and serve in a tall glass.

PIÑA COLADA

My all-time favourite, invented in Puerto Rico, and literally translated as "strained pineapple". The classic recipe suggests coconut cream in place of Malibu, but I love the added zing of the latter. It doesn't include cream either, but I find cream gives a wicked richness to the drink (notwithstanding the extra calories). For a thicker texture, use tinned pineapple chunks instead of juice.

Serves 1
2cl (²/3 fl oz) white rum
2cl (²/3 fl oz) pineapple juice
2cl (²/3 fl oz) Malibu
2cl (²/3 fl oz) fresh double cream
crushed ice

Mix all ingredients in a blender and serve with slices of fresh pineapple and maraschino cherries.

The Undersecretary understates:
"A Bacardi Old Fashioned? It's colossal, stupendous, epic!"

French Delegate denies: *"No! Paris has nothing to compare with a Bacardi Cuba Libre!"*

Suez Savant suffers: *"I actually doubted a Bacardi Punch could be so perfect. Is my fez red!"*

"Hot stuff!" says Chile Consultant...
"A Bacardi Hot Milk Punch has a flavor that warms my heart!"

GREEN PARROT
Visually stunning!

Serves 1
1cl (^{1}/$_3$ fl oz) dark rum
4cl (1 ^{1}/$_3$ fl oz) orange juice
1cl (^{1}/$_3$ fl oz) blue curaçao

Take a large stemmed glass and slowly pour in the ingredients one at a time in the above order. Do not mix. Garnish with orange slices.

AND AN ODDBALL...

HOME-MADE MARROW "RUM"
With special thanks to Margaret "Mum" Schroeder

1 large green marrow
demerara sugar

Take one very large green marrow and cut about an inch off the top. Don't throw this away – keep it in the fridge for use later. Scoop out the flesh and seeds and discard. Now pack the inside with demerara sugar and leave overnight. The sugar will "melt", so top up with more demerara and leave overnight again. Continue doing this until you can't possibly squeeze in any more sugar.

Replace the reserved top and seal it with sticky tape. Put the marrow into a net (or stocking) and suspend it, taped end up, for six to eight weeks. It's best to hang it over a large bowl or jug in case it leaks. It's ready to drain when you can make an indentation in the outside of the marrow with your finger. To drain, pierce a small hole in the base and twice strain the liquid through muslin (or another stocking) before decanting into sterilised bottles. Do not cork the bottles at this stage as the liquid will continue to ferment for a few more weeks.

When you're happy that fermentation is complete, seal the bottles with plastic corks and store upright in a cool place for one year to mature. Yes, you need patience!

To quote Margaret, "It's best to drink this lying down – it saves you the bother of falling down afterwards!".

CHAPTER SEVEN

RUM IN THE KITCHEN

There are zillions of recipes, sweet and savoury, where rum is a fundamental ingredient simply because it's so versatile. Dark rum gives a very pungent flavour to sauces and cakes, for instance, while white rum is the perfect perker-upper for a fruit salad. Try substituting rum for brandy – it works remarkably well. You can even jazz up a serving of humble baked beans by adding some black treacle and a dash (or two!) of dark rum.

Many traditional rum-based recipes have their roots firmly planted in the Caribbean, but its rich and varied cultural heritage means that styles of cuisine have been influenced by the Spanish, the Dutch and the British amongst many others. My personal favourites, however, hail from the

Left
Loading a schooner with coconuts, Kingston, Jamaica.

French islands; I love the fusion of classic French culinary austerity with the bold, exotic, sunshine-filled ingredients and flavours of the tropics.

I could fill an entire book with recipes but will limit myself here to a sumptuous dinner party menu instead…rum-soaked, of course!

STARTER
CRABES FARCIS

The Caribbean is awash with seafood and recipes that use it. Stuffed crabs are a popular dish, with the nuances of the filling varying from island to island. In keeping with our French theme, this recipe comes from Martinique.

Serves 6

500g (1 lb) crabmeat (fresh or canned)
75g (3 oz) fresh white breadcrumbs
1 small chilli, de-seeded and finely chopped
3 tablespoons chives
2 tablespoons chopped parsley
2 garlic cloves, crushed
1 tablespoon fresh lime juice
3 tablespoons good dark rum
25g (1 oz) butter
salt and pepper to taste

Place two-thirds of the breadcrumbs with all the other ingredients except the butter in a food processor and blend until smooth.

If using fresh crab, stuff the shells with this

mixture. Alternatively, use lightly greased scallop shells or ramekin dishes. Sprinkle the remaining breadcrumbs over the top, dot with butter and bake at 175°C/350°F/Gas Mark 4 for about 30 minutes.

MAIN COURSE
BIFTECK À LA CRÉOLE

An incredibly simple way of transforming plain rump steak into a gourmet's delight. Any good dark rum will do and the recipe is equally scrumptious with any other cut of steak. Use individual steaks if you want lots of flavour; for a more subtle style, buy, marinade and cook the steak in one piece, carving it after the flambé stage.

Serves 6

2 tablespoons olive oil
2 tablespoons red wine vinegar
2 garlic cloves, crushed
salt and pepper to taste
6 tablespoons dark rum
1.25kg (3 lbs) rump steak

Mix together the oil, vinegar, garlic and seasoning. Add the steak and leave to marinade for at least four hours, turning it occasionally and basting it with the mixture.

Under a preheated grill, cook the steak for as little or as long as desired, basting it with the leftover marinade.

Transfer it to a warmed plate along with the juices in the bottom of the grill pan.

Warm the rum slightly, pour it over the steak and then put a match to it. Serve the steak as soon as the flames die down.

PUDDING

BANANES À LA MARTINIQUAISE

Rum and banana are a marriage made in flavour heaven! Fritters made from bananas soaked in rum (better still with a dash of rum in the batter, too) are classic, but this pudding, which can be served hot or cold, is a slightly lighter way to round off a meal, especially if you choose to use white rum.

peeled bananas (allow two per person)
brown sugar to taste
pinch ground cloves
juice of half a lemon
1\2 dessertspoon of rum per banana

Put the bananas in a pan and sprinkle them with the sugar and cloves. Add the lemon juice and rum and then just enough water to cover them.

Simmer gently for about 20 minutes or until the bananas are cooked.

**Top Ten Markets
by Volume 1996**

	Million Litres
Philippines	82.0
USA	79.2
India	58.8
Mexico	58.5
Germany	31.8
Canada	22.0
Brazil	14.0
France	13.1
UK	12.8
Spain	7.2

Source: Euromonitor

**Top Ten Markets
by Value 1997**

	US$ Million
USA	1,867
Germany	427
Philippines	380
Canada	369
UK	319
France	170
India	159
Brazil	144
Mexico	134
Italy	74

Source: Euromonitor

**Top Five Markets by
Per Capita Expenditure 1996**

	US$
Canada	12.44
US	7.03
Philippines	5.51
UK	5.47
Germany	5.24

Source: Euromonitor

**World Rum Brands
By Volume Sales 1996**

	Million litres
Bacardi	177.8
Tanduay	90.0
Captain Morgan	18.9
Castillo	12.8
Santa Teresa Gran Reserva	12.2
Cacique	10.8

INDEX

BIBLIOGRAPHY

Barty-King, H. & Massel, A., *Rum Yesterday & Today* (William Heinemann Ltd, 1983)

Hamilton, E., *The Complete Guide To Rum* (Triumph Books, 1997)

Jolly, R. & Willson, T., *Jackspeak – The Pusser's Rum Guide To Royal Navy Slanguage* (Palamanando, 1988)

Pack, J., *Nelson's Blood – The Story Of Naval Rum* (Alan Sutton Publishing Ltd, 1982)

ACKNOWLEDGMENTS

My name may be on the cover but the really hard work was done by all the people who responded with great kindness, friendliness and nothing less than sheer fortitude to my barrage of correspondence. Thank you to everyone who sent information, illustrations and bottles, especially to those who delivered things personally.

I am also amazed and touched by the trust put in me by those who loaned precious, and in some cases irreplaceable, picture material. The list below simply doesn't do justice to the individuals involved but your names are inscribed on my soul!

I owe extra special thanks to my editor at Prion, Andrew Goodfellow, and my husband, John Arkell, both of whom possess a degree of patience never before encountered in mankind. And to the Grant family, who so willingly assisted in lengthy experiments to determine the precise amount of cachaça to use in a *caipirinha*, I simply say "Tranquillo!"

My thanks to:

African Distillers Limited
Alberta Distillers Limited
All India Distillers
  Association
Allied Domecq Spirits &
  Wine (UK) Limited
Angostura Company
  Limited
Anguilla Tourist Board
Aruba Tourism Authority
Association of Canadian
  Distillers
Australian Trade
  Commission
Australian Wine Bureau
Bacardi-Martini Limited
Bacardi Museum
Bahamas Tourist
  Authority
J. Bally
Barbados Tourism Office
Belize Tourist Board
Bernstein Hounsfield
  Associates
BG & Vinceremos
  LimitedBorder Wine
  Merchants

Bourgognes & Domaines
  Michel Picard
British Virgin Islands
  Tourist Board
Bryant Jackson
  Communications
Bundaberg Distilling
  Company Rty Limited
BV Distillerie Smeets
Campbell Distillers
  Limited
Cayman Islands Tourist
  Board
Cellars International
  Limited
Corby Distillers Limited
Ian Crawford
CWS Limited
David Kitchen Marketing
Demerara Distillers
  Limited
Domaine Les Pailles
Dovetail Consultancy
  Services
Eaux de Vie Limited
Euroglen Services Limited
Michael Fogg

Frederic Robinson
  Limited
Gibson International plc
Guinness Northern
  Ireland
Guyana High
  Commission
Halewood International
  Limited
Hall & Bramley Limited
Hammond PR
Heaven Hill Distilleries
  Inc
Highland Merchant
  Company
Petr Hlousek
Hollywood & Donnelly
  Limited
Andy Hopkins
InSpirit Marketing
International Distillers &
  Vintners (UK) Limited
International Distillers
  Kenya Limited
International Distillers
  Uganda Limited
Jamaica Tourist Board

Andrew Jefford
Jim Beam Brands (Greater
    Europe) plc
J J Le Sueur
Andrea Johannová
Kittling Ridge Estate
    Wines & Spirits
Kratz & Company Inc.
La Mauny
Lang Brothers Limited
C Le Masurier Limited
Leestown Company
London Print Matters
    Limited
Ian MacLeod & Company
    Limited
Magnet Harlequin
Malcolm Cowen Limited
Marblehead Brand
    Development Limited
Mauritius Tourist Board
Milsol Distribution
Ministry of Agriculture,
    Fisheries and Food
NBPR
Oddbins Limited
J C & R H Palmer
    Limited
Pernod Ricard Group
Peter Mielzynski Agencies
    Limited
Point of Choice
Rémy & Associates (UK)
    Limited

Rhums Clément
Safeway plc
Sainsbury's Supermarkets
    Limited
San Miguel Corporation
Sazerac Company Inc
Schlümberger KG
Margaret Schroeder
Seagram UK Limited
Serenus International
Sikkim Distilleries
    Limited
Slaur Chauvet SA
A Smith Bowman
    Distillery
Somerfield Stores
St. Austell Brewery
    Company Limited
St. Vincent & The
    Grenadines Tourist
    Office
Tarac Australia Pty.
    Limited
Tesco Stores Limited
The Camerons Brewery
    Company
The Civilized Explorer
The Distillers Company
The Grosvenor Wine &
    Spirit Company Limited
The Main Rum Company
    Limited
The Thresher Group
The Victoria Wine

Company Limited
The West Indies Rum
    Distillery Limited
The Wine & Spirit
    Association
The Wine & Spirit
    Education Trust
    Limited
Charles Tobias, The
    Pusser's Rum Company
Trinidad Tourist Board
Turnround System
    Graphics
Twelve Islands Shipping
    Company Limited
United Distillers &
    Vintners (UDV)
United Distillers
United States Virgin
    Islands Tourism Office
Waverley Vintners
    Limited
West Indies Rum
    Distillery Limited
Westbay Distributors
    Limited
William Cadenhead
    Limited
Winerite Limited
J. Wray & Nephew
    Limited
Ypióca Agroindustrial
    Ltda.

PICTURE ACKNOWLEDGMENTS

The Advertising Archives, London 38, 78, 117, 156
The Al Fayed Archives 49
Mary Evans Picture Library 11, 13, 14-5, 20, 51, 61, 63, 67, 75,
    133, 164-5
The Vintage Magazine Company 22, 96, 176